LGBTQ YOUTH IN FOSTER CARE

Representing an often overlooked population in social work literature, this book explores the experiences of LGBTQ youth as they navigate the child welfare system. Adam McCormick examines the entirety of a youth's experience, from referral into care and challenges to obtaining permanency, to aging out or leaving care. Included throughout the book are stories from LGBTQ youth that address personal issues such as abuse, bullying and harassment, and double standards. Filled with resources to foster resilience and empower youth, this book is ideal for professionals who are hoping to create a more inclusive and affirming system of care for LGBTQ youth.

Adam McCormick, PhD, MSSW, is an assistant professor of social work at St. Edward's University. He teaches courses in child welfare and social work with families.

LGBTQ YOUTH IN FOSTER CARE

Empowering Approaches for an Inclusive System of Care

Adam McCormick

Routledge
Taylor & Francis Group

NEW YORK AND LONDON

First published 2018
by Routledge
711 Third Avenue, New York, NY 10017

and by Routledge
2 Park Square, Milton Park, Abingdon, Oxon, OX14 4RN

Routledge is an imprint of the Taylor & Francis Group, an informa business

© 2018 Taylor & Francis

Library of Congress Cataloging-in-Publication Data
Names: McCormick, Adam, editor.
Title: LGBTQ youth in foster care: empowering approaches for an inclusive system of care / [edited by] Adam McCormick.
Description: Routledge: New York, 2018. | Includes bibliographical references.
Identifiers: LCCN 2018002847 | ISBN 9781138859531 (hardcover: alk. paper) | ISBN 9781138859517 (pbk.: alk. paper) | ISBN 9781315717159 (e-book)
Subjects: LCSH: Sexual minority youth—United States. | Sexual minority youth—Psychology—United States. | Foster home care—United States.
Classification: LCC HQ76.27.Y68 L67 2018 | DDC 306.760835—dc23
LC record available at https://lccn.loc.gov/2018002847

ISBN: 978-1-138-85953-1 (hbk)
ISBN: 978-1-138-85951-7 (pbk)
ISBN: 978-1-315-71715-9 (ebk)

Typeset in Baskerville
by codeMantra

TABLE OF CONTENTS

1

LGBTQ YOUTH IN CARE
Overlooked and Underestimated

Jason

Jason was referred to the foster care system when he was just 11 years old. Jason's referral was unique because unlike most other child welfare cases, the state did not come in and take Jason away from his biological family. There was no suspected history of any type of physical or sexual abuse. In fact, up until that point in time, Jason had never experienced any form of neglect or abuse. Part of what makes Jason's case so unique is not even that he was one of the few children in care whose family members contacted children's protective services and requested that they take custody of Jason Although it is rare, child welfare professionals do receive requests from a child's immediate caretakers to intervene and take custody of the child from time to time. The reasons for these referrals usually occur when a child's caretaker feels that they are unable to provide adequate care to a child or when a child has emotional and behavioral concerns that exceed the capacity of their caretakers. Jason's case was unique because it did not involve any of these dynamics. In fact, when his grandmother was asked by a child protective services investigator why she would no longer care for him, she simply stated that he just didn't fit in with her family and that she refused to allow him to stay in her home any longer. She never expressed any concerns about his behaviors being too much for herself and her husband to handle. Jason never exhibited any emotional or behavioral challenges beyond what was developmentally appropriate for an 11-year old. Both she and her husband were still committed to caring for Jason's younger siblings; therefore, there were no concerns about their ability to provide care.

Jason would eventually go into foster care at the request of his grandparents. Over the course of the next five years, he would have seven different placements, some in traditional foster family homes and some in group homes, and at each one a request would be made for Jason to be removed. He never exhibited any of the risky behaviors that are often exhibited by kids who experience numerous placement breakdowns. He was never suspended from school, never initiated a physical confrontation, and never reported any suicidal or homicidal ideations. In fact, he recalls that most of the time when he would ask why he was being moved, his caseworkers would simply attribute it to his inability to fit in.

By the time he was approaching his 16th birthday, Jason had finally established some stability in a group home for teenage boys. After living in this placement for nearly a year, Jason sat his group home parents down one evening and told them that he was gay. Jason described the moments leading up to this encounter as one of the scariest experiences of his life. He would later describe the overall experience as one of the most empowering and liberating experiences that he would ever have. Jason's group home parents responded with an enormous sense of sensitivity and affirmation. They praised Jason for his courage and assured him that they would do everything that they could to make sure that his experiences would be no different than any of the other boys in the home.

On the heels of this empowering experience, Jason would approach the Director of his group, a gentleman who Jason had developed a very close relationship with, and he would again come out. Jason would not experience the same affirmation and sensitivity this time. In fact, the Director immediately told Jason how disappointed he was in Jason. He would go on to tell Jason that being gay was an abomination and inconsistent with the values of the faith-based foster care agency that supervised Jason's group home. The Director would discourage Jason from mentioning this to anyone else and was very clear that if he mentioned this "gay phase" to anyone else, he would risk losing his placement. Jason went several weeks without telling anyone about this encounter. He would eventually confide in a school counselor about the interaction with the Director. The school counselor, with the best of intentions, phoned the group home Director to voice some of the concerns that she had with his response to Jason's coming out. A few days later, Jason arrived at his group home after school to find his caseworker sitting on the front porch with all of his belongings packed tightly into a duffle bag. He would learn that the Director of the group home had submitted an emergency request for his removal. The Director cited Jason's inability to respect the values of the agency as the reason for his removal. Over the course of the next three years, Jason would bounce from placement to placement, living in group homes, foster homes, and emergency shelters, until he eventually aged out of care on his 18th birthday. He was admitted into a transitional living program and would begin a new journey navigating the system as a homeless young adult.

Jason's story was chosen to provide an introduction into the experiences of LGBTQ youth in the child welfare due in large part to the numerous themes present in his experience that many LGBTQ youth experience as they navigate the child welfare system. From his pathway into care, his experiences while in foster care, to his exit from the system, Jason's story sheds light on the many challenges the child welfare system has in its capacity to provide safe, affirming, and accepting care to LGBTQ youth.

Until recent years, little attention has been given to the experiences of LGBTQ youth who come into contact with the child welfare system. Historically, child welfare practitioners, policy makers, and foster parents have failed to recognize the presence of LGBTQ youth on their caseloads and in foster homes. Recent efforts aimed at exploring the experiences of LGBTQ youth who come into contact with the child welfare system suggest that a number of barriers and challenges exist in creating a safe and affirming environment for LGBTQ youth.

Overrepresentation of LGBTQ Youth in the Child Welfare System

It is estimated that LGBTQ youth are disproportionately overrepresented in the foster care system; however, the exact number of LGBTQ youth in the system is unknown (Mallon, 2006). In a recent study of youth in the California foster care system, 13.6% of foster youth identified as lesbian, gay, bisexual, or questioning and 13.2% reported some level of same-sex attraction. Furthermore, in this same study, 5.6% of respondents identified as transgender (Wilson, Cooper, Kastanis, & Nezhad, 2014).

The reasons that so many LGBTQ youth come into contact with child welfare professionals might often seem unrelated to sexual orientation, gender identity, or expression (SOGIE); however, upon closer examination, these reasons usually have a great deal to do with a child's sexual orientation or gender identity (Mallon, 2011). While the child welfare system is designed to assure safety and security for children and youth who are at the risk of experiencing further maltreatment, the experiences of LGBTQ youth in care are often saturated with further maltreatment, discrimination, and marginalization. Similarly, little emphasis is placed on issues of permanency-related services for LGBTQ youth, such as family reunification, adoption, and legal guardianship. LGBTQ youth are significantly more likely to age out of foster care than straight youth; thus, their transition into adulthood is often faced with numerous challenges and barriers.

The following chapters will provide further insight into the experiences of LGBTQ youth who come into contact with the child welfare system. The stories and experiences of many LGBTQ youth will be shared in an attempt to help put a face on a population that has largely been overlooked and underestimated. After interviewing numerous LGBTQ youth and young adults who have navigated the child welfare system, the author has concluded that this is a population that has an enormous sense of resilience and resourcefulness. Furthermore, the author firmly believes that providing a voice for individuals like Jason and many other LGBTQ youth is an effective mechanism for better understanding the challenges and barriers that exist in creating an affirming and inclusive child welfare system for all children and youth.

Language and Terminology

The words and terminology that are used when working with LGBTQ youth in care can have a profound impact on their sense of comfort and safety. Given the fact that many LGBGT youth have had previous negative experiences around issues related to their sexual orientation or gender identity, they are often looking for signs or indications from child welfare professionals and caretakers that are sensitive and affirming. The use of language that is competent and sensitive can create a more inclusive culture in which LGBTQ youth can be themselves. The remainder of the chapter seeks to provide some basic terminology and language for child welfare professionals and caretakers to possess to enhance and strengthen their interactions with LGBTQ youth.

SOGIE

SOGIE is an acronym that stands for sexual orientation, gender identity and gender expression. When working with youth in the child welfare system, it's important to remember that all youth have a SOGIE, and much like race and ethnicity, a youth's SOGIE is an important piece of their identity.

Sexual Orientation

Sexual orientation is the desire for intimate emotional and/or physical relationships with another person. The terms heterosexual and homosexual were historically used in referring to an individual's sexual orientation; however, those terms are largely discouraged because they reduce a youth's identity to purely sexual terms. When discussing issues related to a youth's sexual orientation, child welfare professionals also want to avoid using the term sexual pref-erence. This type of language suggests that being gay is somehow a choice and can be changed or modified in some way. Terms such as gay, lesbian, and bisexual are much af-firming and sensitive to use when discussing a youth's sex-ual orientation.

As families and society become more accepting of LGBTQ individuals, the average age for youth to come out as gay, lesbian, or bisexual has dropped significantly. In the 1980s, the average coming out age was 22 as compared to today where the average coming out age is 16. According to a recent Pew survey, the average age at which LGBTQ indi-viduals first noticed that they were something other than straight was around 12 years.

Gender Identity and Expression

A person's gender identity can be viewed as their internal sense of being masculine or feminine. The term trans-gender is often used as an umbrella term for individuals whose gender identity (internal sense of gender) is differ-ent from their assigned gender. When working with trans-gender youth, child welfare professionals should always seek to use a transgender youth's chosen name and chosen use of pronouns consistent with the gender they identify with. In cases where a youth uses certain pronouns when referring to themselves, it is important that child welfare professionals mirror that language to the best of their abil-ity. Furthermore, making it a habit to ask youth what their preferred pronouns are can be effective in modeling re-spect and cultural competence. When youth are referred to with the wrong pronouns, they may feel disrespected, aligned, or dismissed. LGBTQ youth often have a height-ened vigilance when meeting new professionals, and the

Table 1.1 **Gender-Inclusive Pronoun Chart**

Traditional Masculine	He sang.	Mom picked him up.	His phone rang.	That is his.	He saved himself.
Traditional Feminine	She sang.	Mom picked her up.	Her phone rang.	That is hers.	She saved herself.
Gender Neutral (They)	They sang.	Mom picked them up.	Their phone rang.	That is theirs.	They saved themself.
Gender Neutral (Ze)	Ze sang.	Mom picked hir up.	Hir phone rang.	That is hirs.	Ze saved hirself.

use of gender-preferred pronouns can potentially provide them some ease. Some common gender-neutral pronouns that child welfare professionals might consider include the following (Table 1.1):

- They/Them/Theirs—This is certainly the most commonly used gender-neutral pronoun and can be used in both the singular and plural.
- Ze/hir—Ze is pronounced like "zee" and is used to replace he/she/they. Hir is pronounced like "here" and replaces her/hers/him/his/they/theirs.

Cisgender is a term that is used to describe someone whose gender identity largely aligns with those typically assigned to their assigned gender. Gender conforming is a reference for individuals who do not behave in a way that conforms to the traditional expectations of their assigned gender. More simply put, gender nonconforming is a term that many individuals prefer when their gender identity and expression do not fit neatly into any one category.

Some youth do not identify as gender binary, a concept describing gender identity as being entirely masculine or feminine. A youth who identifies as gender variant likely does not conform to the societal constructs or expectations related to gender. Some gender-variant youth might identify as genderqueer, in which they don't identify as either male or female, but rather a combination of the two genders.

The terminology and concepts related to SOGIE are very fluid and consistently evolving. Many child welfare professionals may feel overwhelmed or confused by the fluidity of these concepts and terms. LGBTQ youth in the child welfare system often feel a sense of frustration with the lack of willingness of child welfare professionals to address and acknowledge issues related to SOGIE. In many cases, LGBTQ youth feel that this reluctance to address issues stems from the discomfort and lack of confidence that child welfare professionals might have when it comes to discussing issues related to SOGIE (McCormick, Schmidt, & Terrazas, 2016). While keeping up with the most sensitive and affirming terminology and language is crucial, it is equally important that child welfare professionals not allow their discomfort or lack of confidence to prevent them from engaging in crucial conversations about a youth's SOGIE. The experiences of LGBTQ youth who navigate the child welfare system provide evidence of the profound negative impact that silence and a lack of acknowledgement can have on their well-being and permanence. In situations where a child welfare professional might lack the necessary knowledge or vocabulary related to a youth's SOGIE, it's important that they remember that it is okay to ask questions.

2

PATHWAYS INTO FOSTER CARE FOR LGBTQ YOUTH

Overrepresentation of LGBTQ Youth

It is unknown just how many LGBTQ youth currently reside in the foster care system. Data assessing a child's sexual orientation or gender identity are not tracked by child welfare agencies. Similarly, many youth in care are reluctant to disclose information about their sexual orientation or gender identity for a number of reasons. Many LGBTQ youth fear that their placements could be in jeopardy or that they may be discriminated against or marginalized if their caretakers were to become aware of their LGBTQ status. Thus, many youth feel that remaining in the closet is safer than being out in their current foster homes. While it is understandable that an LGBTQ youth would opt to not disclose certain information as a way to protect themself as they navigate the foster care experience, it is a dynamic that should be very concerning for child welfare professionals.

Recent efforts to assess the benefits of being out suggest that youth who are out to their caretakers have significantly higher rates of self-esteem and life satisfaction than those who are not. Similarly, LGBTQ youth who come out to their loved ones or caretakers are much less likely to be depressed (Russell, Toomey, Ryan, & Diaz, 2014). Furthermore, we have known for some time that teens who are forced to keep their identities a secret are at an increased risk of depression, suicidal ideation, risky sexual behaviors, and suicidal behaviors (Ryan, Huebner, Diaz, & Sanches, 2009). Many LGBTQ youth in care go to incredible lengths to keep their identities a secret.

Jennifer

Jennifer described the immense amount of energy and planning that she devoted to keeping her identity a secret from her longtime foster parents: "From the time I woke up in the morning until the time that I went to bed I would do everything that I could to make sure that they wouldn't know. I would delete texts, pretend that I had boyfriends, and make sure that none of my teachers knew anything because X (foster mom) emailed my teachers everyday. It's a lot more work than what you would imagine."

In a recent survey of youth aged 12–21 in the California foster care system, 19.1% of respondents identified as LGBTQ (Wilson, Cooper, Kastanis, & Nezhad, 2014). In this same study, nearly a quarter (22.2%) of respondents aged 17–21 identified as LGBTQ. Therefore, the rate of LGBTQ youth living in foster care is nearly twice the rate of LGBTQ youth in the general population.

Many LGBTQ youth enter the child welfare system for the same reasons as straight youth. There are, however, a number of explanations that help us to better understand why so many LGBTQ youth end up in the foster care system. The experiences of LGBTQ youth who come into contact with the child welfare system often differ significantly from the experiences of straight youth. The reasons that an LGBTQ youth is referred to the child welfare system often look much different from those of straight youth. Although at first glance they might seem like they have nothing to do with a youth's SOGIE, after further examination, those reasons often have much to do with issues pertaining to a youth's SOGIE. A little under half of LGBTQ youth in state custody (44%) report that they were either removed or kicked out of their homes for issues related to their sexual orientation or gender identity (Ryan & Diaz, 2005).

Many LGBTQ youth enter the child welfare system for many of the same reasons as straight youth. In the interviews with LGBTQ youth that were conducted for this book it was uncommon for youth to enter care for reasons related to some combination of poverty, parental mental illness, and/ or substance abuse in the family. The disproportionate overrepresentation of LGBTQ youth in the child welfare system, however, is largely explained by dynamics that can be directly attributed to a youth's SOGIE. LGBTQ youth are much more likely to be referred to child welfare services for issues such as hostility in the family, running away from home, abandonment by their parents or caretakers, and school truancy. While these pathways into care may initially seem completely unrelated to a youth's SOGIE, we learn very quickly after hearing from youth, that in most cases their SOGIE had everything to do with why they came into contact with the child welfare system.

Physical and Sexual Abuse

While most LGBTQ youth never experience physical or sexual abuse, research suggests that LGBTQ youth in general are at an increased risk of experiencing physical and sexual violence (CDC, 2011). Risks of physical and sexual abuse are among the most common reasons for child welfare intervention. Sexual minority youth are nearly three times more likely to report childhood experiences of sexual abuse when compared to other adolescents. LGBTQ youth also 1.3 times more likely to report experiencing physical abuse from their parents than straight and gender conforming youth (Friedman et al., 2011).

In a groundbreaking study on the maltreatment experiences of gender nonconforming youth, researchers found that children who do not display gender conformity in things such as dress, play, and interests are significantly more likely to experience physical, sexual, and psychological abuse (Roberts, Rosario, Corliss, Koenen, & Austin, 2012a). Boys in the study who displayed gender nonconformity were nearly three times more likely to experience sexual abuse at some point during their childhood than boys who were gender typical. Similarly, gender nonconforming girls were nearly 60% more likely to be sexually abused during their childhood than their gender-conforming counterparts. The rates of posttraumatic stress disorder in young adults in this same study who exhibited gender nonconforming behaviors as children were nearly double that of those who did not.

Hostility and Rejection in the Family

Family rejection and hostility related to a youth's sexual orientation or gender identity largely contribute to the overrepresentation of LGBTQ youth in care. LGBTQ youth are kicked out of their homes or run away from their homes at rates significantly higher than straight youth. According to a recent study, homeless LGBTQ youth represent nearly 40% of all youth who are on the streets (Durso & Gates, 2012).

The conflict and tension that stems from a parent's rejection of their child's sexual orientation or gender identity often serves as a catalyst for a child's involvement with the courts. Prosecutors often file charges on LGBTQ youth for being "incorrigible", a charge that suggests that their behaviors are out of the control of their caretakers. Such charges lead to criminalization of LGBTQ youth and often result in placement in foster care.

Nick

Nick was 16 when a child welfare investigator showed up at his school. Although he still doesn't know who contacted child welfare services with concerns about his safety and well-being, Nick is pretty sure that it was a teacher or school counselor. Over the course of just a few months in the spring semester of his sophomore year of high school, Nick's school attendance and performance had drastically changed for the worse. He was missing two or three days of school a week and failing almost all of his coursework. A school truancy officer was the first to approach Nick about his problems at school. Nick was then referred to a school guidance counselor. Nick confided in the counselor and explained that his parents had told him that he was no longer welcome in their home after learning that he had been in a romantic relationship with another boy from his school. Nick had been staying with different friends, often without their parents knowing. He had slept in garages, backyards, and bathtubs. He went on to explain that he was staying with a friend across town and that finding a ride to school was very difficult; thus, he was missing school regularly and had fallen behind in his coursework.

After meeting with child welfare professionals, Nick would mention that his parents, at the advice of their pastor, refused to acknowledge Nick until he was no longer a "practicing homosexual". The pastor instructed them that this "tough love" was the only way to stop his behavior and that any efforts to accept Nick would only further enable him to engage in "homosexual

*behavior". Nick would tell child welfare investigators that he
had made numerous attempts to try to reconcile with his parents; however, they refused to speak to him as long as he was
gay. Nick would eventually enter the foster care system and be
placed in a group home in the neighboring town.*

What makes Nick's pathway into care so unique from that
of many straight youth is that his family had very few risk
factors that are often present in many families that come
into contact with the child welfare system. Common caretaker risk factors associated with child welfare referrals include poverty, parental mental illness, parental substance
abuse, and housing instability. At the time of his referral,
Nick's family had none of these risk factors. They were a
middle-class family who had lived in the same home since
before he was born. Neither of his parents ever abused any
substances, including alcohol, and he was unaware of any
major mental illness in the family.

School to Foster Care Pipeline

The initial referrals for many LGBTQ youth in foster care
can be traced back to issues that they experienced in their
schools. According to the most recent climate study conducted by the Gay, Lesbian and Straight, Education Network (Kosciw, Greytak, Palmer, & Boesen, 2013), LGBTQ
youth continue to face very unsafe and threatening school
environments. Nearly three-quarters of LGBTQ youth
report experiencing some form of verbal harassment at
school (74%) and just under one-third (30%) missed
school for fears related to their safety at school. Furthermore, nearly one-third of LGBTQ youth who drop out
of school report that they do so in an attempt to avoid
harassment.

LGBTQ youth are often at an increased risk of being disciplined and suspended from school. In seminal study assessing the academic experiences of LGBTQ youth, researchers found that gay and transgender youth are nearly three times more likely than straight youth to experience harsh disciplinary treatment by school administrators (Mitchum & Moodie Mills, 2014). Although LGBTQ youth in this same study were much more likely to be the victims, rather than the aggressors, in instances of school conflict, they are much more likely to receive harsh discipline than their straight counterparts. This trend is alarming due in large part to the fact that multiple school suspensions increase a student's likelihood of eventually dropping out of school by nearly five times. LGBTQ youth are often referred to truancy officers, school social workers, and school resource officers, which places them at an increased risk of child welfare referral.

Letty

Letty described herself as "your typical C student" before peers at her school learned that she was in a Lesbian relationship with a classmate. Letty started to receive verbal harassment from some of the kids at her school. They called her "dyke" and "butch". Many of her close friends started to distance themselves from her, and her best friend's mother restricted her daughter from being around Letty. While all of these things caused distress for Letty, it wasn't until a few of her male classmates started to sexually harass and threaten her that she would begin missing school and skipping certain class periods as a way to protect herself. Two classmates approached her in the hallway after school on multiple occasions and made comments suggesting that they could do things to her sexually that would "turn her straight again". On one occasion, one of the boys tried pulling her into the bathroom. School was no longer a safe place for Letty. She started skipping the classes that she had with the students who were harassing her. She eventually started missing entire days of school. Letty's truancy case was later referred to the courts, and her mother and stepfather agreed to have her voluntarily placed at a children's group home that specialized in behavioral issues. Letty would have a romantic relationship with one of the girls in one of the neighboring cottages on the campus. Both girls would be asked to leave; however, Letty's mother and step father refused to come pick her up, an incident that would lead to an investigation by children's protective services and a subsequent foster care placement. While Letty's referral with children's protective services cites tension with her caretakers, behavioral issues, school truancy, and parental abandonment as the reason for her entry into foster care, many of those issues were strongly related to the tension and hostility associated with her being a lesbian.

Conclusion

Understanding the differences in the experiences and pathways into care for LGBTQ youth is critical for child welfare professionals. These experiences largely predict what child welfare interventions are most appropriate and offer the best chances for establishing permanency. A sensitive and culturally competent assessment that takes into consideration the role that things like rejection, bullying, and risk related to a youth's sexual orientation and gender identity have played allows for child welfare professionals to begin creating a plan of action that is inclusive and affirming. At a time when the child welfare system has begun to stress the individuality and uniqueness of children and youth, understanding the unique pathways into care that many LGBTQ youth have found themselves on will only help professionals to better identify the most appropriate services and interventions to assist youth and their families. Additionally, it is critical that child welfare professionals understand that services and interventions for LGBTQ may look markedly different from those for straight youth. For instance, more traditional child welfare services such as substance abuse treatment, mental health services, and parenting classes may not be as effective as psychoeducational interventions addressing the role that family acceptance plays, as well as intensive family therapy to address tension, hostility, and rejection in the family unit.

3

EXPERIENCES IN CARE FOR LGBTQ YOUTH

When placing a youth in out-of-home care, the public child welfare system is ultimately responsible for ensuring the safety and protection of that youth. At its core, child protection services are designed to ensure that children are placed in settings that offer the least amount of risk to a youth as possible. When the decision is made to place a child in out-of-home care, that placement is intended to present as little risk of harm to a youth as possible. The experiences of many LGBTQ youth in out-of-home care, however, suggest that out-of-home care placement can be a very risky and dangerous place. In many cases, their experiences are much more risky and dangerous than what they might have faced prior to entering care.

When we look at factors that are often considered to be associated with positive experiences in out-of-home care for youth, we quickly realize that LGBTQ youth often encounter a number of disparities in their experiences. A number of protective factors have been identified that are associated with more positive experiences for youth in out-of-home care. These factors include things like protection from abuse and violence; permanency and stability in living arrangements; supportive social networks; positive self-identity; and adequate services to meet a youth's mental, spiritual, and physical health needs. The experiences of LGBTQ youth provide insight into the fact that the child welfare system has failed in many ways to protect LGBTQ youth.

Lack of Acknowledgement

The child welfare system has historically been unwilling to acknowledge the presence of LGBTQ youth (Mallon, 1998). There is no question that this lack of acknowledgement is largely responsible for many of the challenges, disparities, and struggles that LGBTQ youth in care face today (Woronoff & Estrada, 2006). Not only has this lack of visibility served to silence LGBTQ youth in many ways, by not acknowledging their presence and the potential challenges, child welfare professionals and policy makers have failed to create a system that addresses potential barriers for LGBTQ youth. This reluctance to acknowledge the presence of LGBTQ youth is especially alarming considering the findings from recent research with LGBTQ young adults that suggest that openness and a willingness to discuss issues of sexual orientation are strongly associated with positive outcomes (Ryan et al., 2009). In qualitative interviews and listening forums across the nation, many LGBTQ youth in care have voiced that they feel pressured to remain invisible and silent. Similarly, many of these same youth express that there is an institutional desire to continue not to acknowledge their presence (Mallon & Woronoff, 2006).

In most states, foster parents and child welfare professionals receive intensive training on numerous topics; however, few states mandate specific training on issues related to SOGIE. The author of this book spends a great deal of time traveling all over the US to conduct trainings for foster parents and child welfare professionals, and most have had very little training specific to issues to SOGIE. Even fewer have been trained on the specific needs of LGBTQ youth in foster care. This lack of accurate and valuable knowledge contributes to a workforce that is uncomfortable and inadequate when it comes to discussing issues related to sexual orientation and gender identity.

Gina

Although Gina's foster mother was clearly upset and uncomfortable with the fact that Gina came out as a lesbian, in the two years that they lived together, the two never had an actual conversation about it. In fact, Gina felt that her foster mother would go to incredible lengths to avoid any form of conversation about anything related to her sexual orientation. When Gina would mention the name of a girl that she had been dating, her foster mother would either change the conversation as quickly as possible or find a reason to leave the room. When discussing the impact that her foster mother's unwillingness to acknowledge these issues, Gina notes the following, "the silence was worse than anything. Sometimes I felt like I just wanted her to say how much it disgusted her or how much she hated it. She wouldn't talk about it and that made me feel even worse about myself. It also made me feel so uncomfortable and unwelcome in that house".

The lack of consciousness about the presence of the LGBTQ population in the child welfare system comes at a time when societal awareness of the presence and needs of the LGBTQ community is at its highest. Furthermore, other systems of care serving youth and young adults appear to have a much greater level of comfort and willingness in acknowledging the presence of LGBTQ youth than the child welfare system. Most notably, runaway and homeless youth programs, which have historically seen a disproportionate overrepresentation of LGBTQ youth accessing services, have made significant strides in creating more affirming and accepting environments (Mallon & Woronoff, 2006).

Lack of Acceptance

A common theme consistent in the experiences of LGBTQ youth in care is a lack of acceptance from their peers and caretakers. Several studies have cited the stories of youth who have been forced to leave their placement or who have run away from their placements due to their caregiver's lack of acceptance (Estrada & Marksmaker, 2006; Mallon, 1998). Many caretakers refuse to allow an LGBTQ youth in their home once they learn of his or her sexual orientation or gender identity. Similarly, many LGBTQ youth experience a significant shift in the way they are treated by their caretaker when their caregivers learn of their sexual orientation or gender identity.

Garrett

Garrett lived in eight different foster placements, including numerous group home placements before he was placed with what he considered to be the perfect foster family. After living with this foster family for nearly 18 months, the family was even beginning to discuss the possibility of adopting Garrett. Garrett had developed an especially close relationship with his foster father. In fact, for the first time in his life, he lived with a man who made him feel safe and loved. One evening Garrett sat down with his foster father and told him that he was gay. Garrett's foster father responded by quoting bible scriptures and informed Garrett that if he wanted to remain with the family, he would have to make a choice as to whether or not he would continue in what his foster father referred to as a "homosexual lifestyle". Garrett commented about the emotional toll that his foster father's response had on him and the manner in which he internalized the shame, confusion, and humiliation: "I couldn't believe it. I didn't know what to expect when I told him, but I definitely didn't expect for him to be so disappointed in me. It was like I felt really angry and confused, but at the same time I felt really worried that I would lose something that I didn't want to lose".

Garrett decided to do everything possible to preserve his placement and convince his foster parents that he was straight. He went to great lengths to show his foster parents that he was attracted to girls. He would invite girls over to the home, go on dates, and would even intentionally leave open emails that he sent to girls in hopes that his foster parents might discover them.

Double Standards

It is very common for LGBTQ youth to experience double standards in which they are not afforded the same rights and privileges as straight youth. Some youth are given consequences, in some cases a loss of placement for things that their straight counterparts would never be questioned about. These double standards are often encountered when an LGBTQ youth engages in a romantic relationship. LGBTQ youth are often prohibited or discouraged from engaging in romantic relationships and dating when straight youth in the same homes are permitted and, in some cases, even encouraged to engage in relationships.

Martha

Martha had a very close relationship with her foster family before she came out to them when she was 16. Martha had always admired the fact that her foster family tried to make her life as normal as possible. She and the other youth in the home were encouraged to go out with friends, go on dates, and to take part in as many extracurricular activities as they wanted. When Martha came out, she said that things changed dramatically. She was no longer encouraged to go out with friends, and on many occasions, she was prohibited from going out at all. Martha's foster siblings mentioned to her on a number of occasions that her foster parents would frequently question them about which of her friends were lesbians. Her foster family showed much less interest in extracurricular interests as they did with the other girls in the home. Martha's foster parents made no secret that while they could not forbid her from engaging in a romantic relationship with her girlfriend, they would not do anything to make the relationship any easier. While Martha's foster siblings were allowed to go on dates and have their straight romantic partners over to the house, Martha was not provided those same privileges. On numerous occasions when she asked if a friend could come over, one time to attend a holiday party, her foster mother said that it depends on whether she was coming over as a friend or a girlfriend.

Matt

On the way to his new foster home in a neighboring town, Matt asked his caseworker if it would be possible for him to see his boyfriend on occasion. His caseworker advised him that she would ask his new foster parents, but she also cautioned him that it is very uncommon for foster parents to transport youth for things like dating regardless of whether they are straight or gay. During the intake meeting with the foster parents, the caseworker mentioned that Matt was in a relationship and that he would like to see if it would be possible to go back to his hometown on occasion to see his boyfriend. His new foster father chuckled and asked the caseworker if she was joking. All of this took place right in front of Matt who was immensely embarrassed at this point. When the caseworker left, she informed Matt that there was nothing that she could do because those decisions are left entirely to the foster parents. Visits were never arranged for Matt to see his boyfriend, who was only 45 minutes away.

Bullying, Teasing, and Harassment

Not only do many LGBTQ youth have to deal with the ways in which reactions to their SOGIE might impact things like placement stability, the manner in which they are treated by caretakers and child welfare professionals, and access to their siblings, many also have to deal with bullying, teasing, and harassment from their peers.

The culture of the child welfare system is viewed by many LGBTQ youth to be one that enables youth, staff, and even professionals to engage in stigmatizing and even homophobic behaviors. LGBTQ youth in group homes and foster homes are often the targets of homophobic slurs, bullying, and even physical and sexual harassment and violence. Negative terms and names about gays and lesbians are often tossed around in homes and shelters with little or no redirection.

Jimmy

Jimmy was placed in numerous group homes, foster homes, shelters, and treatment centers. In fact, he said that he had lost count of how many different places he'd lived while he was in care, but estimated that it was probably more than 20. Jimmy notes that there is nothing that brings out the worst in other kids in care than being around someone who is different, especially someone who is gay. He states: "It's like I could see the relief on the faces of the other kids in my placements who were probably picked on and bullied when I would arrive. They knew that I would get teased and messed with more than they would. I got to where I would make it very clear that I was gay as soon as I got in a new place just so I could get it over with".

Blame for Maltreatment

Many LGBTQ youth report they have been disciplined or in many cases even blamed for the maltreatment and harassment that they experienced from peers in the home and at school. Caretakers, teachers, caseworkers, and others often credit an LGBTQ youth's insistence on discussing their romantic relationships or any other issues related to their sexual orientation or gender identity for the harassment, teasing, and other maltreatment that they experience from their peers. Similarly, the experiences of many LGBTQ youth suggest that caretakers are often more inclined to blame LGBTQ youth for their mistreatment than they are to intervene and provide consequences to the perpetrators.

Curtis

Curtis woke one morning to find that his roommates had written the word "faggot" on many of his belongings while he was asleep. Before leaving for school, he explained to his foster mother what his roommates had done and showed her some of his books and CDs that had been vandalized. Before he could even finish telling her the story, she immediately minimized the behaviors of his roommates and attributed the behaviors to the discomfort that they had with that fact that Curtis insisted on talking about his boyfriend. She continued to caution him about talking about his relationships and to consider how uncomfortable it made the other kids feel. Curtis went on to describe the ways in which this incident contributed to his decision to run away from this foster home a few days later: "I knew that this wasn't a place that I could stay. It's one thing to have kids mess with you and not want to have anything to do with you. I was openly gay in foster care for a long time and I could handle that, but when your staff or foster parents aren't willing to stop the kids from bullying you that is when you know that it's time to go".

Valerie

Valerie approached her caseworker about the fact that some of the other kids in her foster group home and at school were leaving her out because they did not feel comfortable with the fact that she was a lesbian. Her caseworker asked her to reflect on the idea that her peers might be on to something. She went on to justify the behaviors of her peers and informed Valerie that her peers were simply displaying tough love and that they weren't going to accept her negative choices. The caseworker refused to approach Valerie's foster parents about the teasing, leaving her to fend for herself in an environment that was hostile and threatening.

Housing in Isolation

Many LGBTQ youth are prevented from sharing bedrooms and bathrooms with other youth for reasons that relate to their SOGIE. For many gay, lesbian, and bisexual youth, their caretakers or foster parents fear that they might engage in romantic or sexual relationships with youth of the same sex, so they isolate them to their own rooms, or in some cases to their own section of the home.

Tina

Tina lived in a group home with seven other teenage girls. She described herself as a kid who just tried to stay under the radar. One evening a staff member who provided weekend relief care for the group home parents found a letter that Tina had written to another girl who lived in the home. The letter had several comments noting Tina's feelings for the other girl and was very flirtatious. Tina asserted that there was no mention anywhere in the letter about anything that pertained to physical relations or desires. When the group home parents returned on Monday morning and learned of this letter, they moved Tina to a room that had been used for storage at the end of a hallway, far removed from all of the other teens in the home. When Tina asked for clarification about why she was being moved from her room and placed in a room alone, her group home parents stated that she could not be trusted with the other girls.

While some youth are isolated to their rooms for fears that they might attempt to initiate physical relations with their same-sex peers, others tell of being isolated for fears for their own safety.

Aaron

When Aaron complained to the staff at his therapeutic foster group home that his peers were engaging in homophobic bullying, harassment, and teasing, the staff members placed him by himself in a room that was supposed to be designated for staff. When he protested this arrangement, his staff members told him that this was the only way that they could assure his safety from his peers.

Pressure to Participate in Gender-Conforming Activities

LGBTQ youth are often pressured to participate in gender-conforming extracurricular activities. Males report being discouraged or prohibited from participating in activities that are perceived as being effeminate, while females are discouraged or prohibited from activities that are more closely associated with masculinity. Similarly, many LGBTQ youth convey that their caretakers exhibit less attention to their interests and extracurricular activities than those of straight youth in foster homes. Participation in things like gay-straight alliances (GSAs), pride festivals, and other LGBTQ-specific programs can have a positive impact on things like self-esteem, school connectedness, social support, family acceptance, and academic performance. For many LGBTQ youth in care, however, their caregivers are unwilling or opposed to their participation in many of these programs. In some cases, youth report that their foster parents or staff are reluctant to provide transportation, and others suggest that their participation in groups or activities that affirm their sexual orientation or gender identity is strictly prohibited.

Ryan

One morning when Ryan was at school, his foster father received a phone call from the state licensing office that an inspector would be out later that day to do a routine home inspection to ensure that the home met all licensing requirements. While cleaning up the bedrooms in preparation for the visit, Ryan's foster father came across Ryan's journal, a gift that his birth mother had given to him for his birthday. That afternoon, moments after the licensing inspector left the home, the foster father invited all of the boys into the living room for a family meeting. He went on to explain that while cleaning the house earlier in the day, he happened to come across Ryan's journal. He pulled the journal out and held it up for each of the boys to see. He proceeded to explain to the boys that journaling and writing about things like feelings, attractions, and relationships were not what young men were supposed to do. He went on to list the things that young men are "supposed" to do, citing things like hunting, wrestling, teasing, playing sports, and many other activities that are often considered to be masculine. He went on to caution the boys that if he finds any of their "fag logs" lying around the house, he would rip them up. He then tore up Ryan's journal in front of the boys. The boys laughed and taunted Ryan for weeks after that. Furthermore, Ryan would go on to explain how this incident impacted his feelings of safety and comfort in this home. The emotional turmoil and subsequent feelings of being isolated and harassed that Ryan experienced on the heels of this incident are evident in his following statement: "I just didn't want to live there anymore. I didn't fit in. It wasn't a safe place for me. It was like he gave them permission to make my life a living hell and they did. I honestly think that he thought that this would make me change and be straight or more manly, but it only made me hate them more and keep to myself".

Reese

A few weeks after she moved into her new group home and started her new school, a classmate invited Reese, who was out at school and in her group home, to attend the GSA meeting that was held immediately after school. Reese knew that her group home parents would likely not agree to allow her to attend the meetings because they had made numerous comments to convey that they weren't comfortable with gays and lesbians. Reese decided to tell them that she was staying after school for some extra tutoring. After a few weeks, her group home parents learned that she was actually staying to attend GSA meetings and informed her that she could no longer stay back after school. Reese protested this decision to her caseworker during a monthly visit and asked that the caseworker advocate for her to attend the meetings. Not only did her caseworker refuse to address the issue with her foster parents, but she also likened Reese's reaction to this decision to other behaviors that Reese exhibited in her previous placement that the caseworker deemed to be antagonistic and attention seeking.

Reparative and Conversion Therapies

Foster parents and caretakers of LGBTQ youth often do everything that they can in an attempt to convert a child's sexual orientation or gender identity. Numerous youth have been forced to see therapists or enter programs aimed at changing a child's sexual orientation, despite the overwhelming evidence noting the negative psychological and social consequences of reparative and conversion interventions. Sexual orientation behavioral change efforts by mental health professionals, commonly referred to as conversion or reparative therapies, developed in the 1960s (SAMHSA, 2015). Survivors of reparative therapies have consistently described the techniques such as treating innate feelings like a mental illness, posing questions and making comments in an attempt to create immense self-doubt, and telling youth that being gay is synonymous with being less of a man or woman. Many professional organizations including the American Psychological Association, American Academy of Pediatrics, and the National Association of Social Workers have taken positions that strongly discourage and condemn the use of reparative therapies, noting that there is no evidence that sexual orientation or gender identity can be modified through therapy. Furthermore, many of these groups have cited the fact that efforts to change LGBTQ youths' sexual orientation or gender identity can decrease their self-esteem, encourage family rejection, and further isolate and marginalize them. A recent study found that lesbian and gay individuals who received religious counseling were more likely to attempt suicide than those who received no counseling at all (Haas, Rodgers, & Herman, 2014).

Efforts to prevent mental health professionals from practicing reparative therapies at the state level have increased dramatically in recent years. While three states currently have laws clearly restricted the use of reparative therapies by licensed mental health professionals, similar legislative proposals have been introduced in 18 other states. These legislative efforts are especially momentous to LGBTQ youth in foster care because foster youth have historically had very little say into their mental health treatment. Child welfare professionals and foster parents have typically been responsible for deciding if mental health treatment is necessary for a youth, and what type of services are most appropriate and who will provide those services.

Ben

Ben was 16 when the biological son of Ben's foster parents told his foster mother that there was a rumor at school that Ben had been in a romantic relationship with another boy. When confronted with this information by his foster parents, Ben confirmed that he had been romantically involved with a young man for a few weeks. Ben's foster parents consulted with the family's pastor, and it was decided that Ben would attend intensive counseling with one of the Christian counselors on staff at the church. It was no secret that the intention of this intervention was to help Ben to understand the sinful nature of this relationship and to encourage him to engage in straight romantic relationships. The counselor made numerous comments that Ben felt were aimed at trying to humiliate and shame him for his feelings. Ben was told that his romantic feelings and physical attraction to other males stem from the early childhood abuse that he suffered. In an attempt to end the counseling sessions, Ben agreed to not engage in any further romantic relationships with young men so long as he lived in this foster home. Ben would eventually make a request to his caseworker to be removed from the home and placed into a group home.

Pressure to Participate in Religious Activities

Amber

Amber was living in a foster home with her two younger siblings. After being separated from her siblings for almost an entire year, Amber was excited to be reunited with them in a long-term placement. Amber did not disclose any information to her new foster family at the time of her placement. While there were a number of things about this placement that Amber appreciated, including having foster parents that she got a long with and attending a school that she liked, Amber's only complaint had to do with the church that the family attended. Each Sunday morning and most Wednesday evenings, the family attended services and Amber was strongly encouraged to participate in youth group activities. Amber became very uncomfortable with the idea of attending this church and taking part in youth group activities because both the pastor and the youth pastor would routinely make negative comments about gays and lesbians in sermons and bible studies. Not only did Amber feel that she wasn't in a safe place to come out to her foster parents and peers, but she also remained silent about her frustrations with the church and youth group for fear that she might disrupt a placement with her siblings. Amber only confided in a few close friends at school and never came out to her foster parents until well after she aged out of care and moved from the home.

The potential risks associated with Amber coming out to her friends and foster parents are very common in the experiences of LGBTQ youth in foster care. Many youth face the reality of things like losing their placements, being separated from siblings, harassment, marginalization, and potential isolation if information about their SOGIE is discovered.

4

PERMANENCY CHALLENGES FOR LGBTQ YOUTH

In addition to protecting children from potential harm, the child welfare system is also responsible for establishing permanency. The process of establishing, maintaining, and achieving permanency for youth in the child welfare system can be a very difficult one. Efforts to provide children with the opportunity to have permanent and stable living situations through family reunification, adoption, supervised guardianship, kinship placement, or other permanent living situations have been given high priority over the past two decades. When deciding the most appropriate plan for permanency, child welfare professionals typically look at the following questions:

1   Were all reasonable efforts made to attempt to reunite the youth with their family of origin?
2   Were all reasonable efforts made to place the youth with their siblings?
3   Were efforts made to try and place the youth in a kinship placement?
4   Were all reasonable efforts made to try and maintain the youth's family connections and relationships?
5   Is the youth in the least restrictive placement possible?

LGBTQ youth are especially vulnerable to many challenges and disparities when it comes to establishing permanency.

The actual permanency outcomes that are achieved for many LGBTQ youth fall far short of what states typically deem to be desirable, and there is little doubt that issues related to sexual orientation gender identity and expression (SOGIE) have a great deal to do with these permanency challenges.

Challenges to Family Reunification

Little emphasis has historically been given to issues of permanency for LGBTQ youth in care. LGBTQ youth in care often have little if any ties to their birth family or home communities. While family support and engagement are usually the starting point in establishing permanency for foster youth, this has not historically been the case for LGBTQ youth. It is important to understand the ways in which things like family rejection, tension, and hostility have contributed to why an LGBTQ youth came into care. The underlying factors that contribute to an LGBTQ youth's referral into care are often much different from what child welfare professionals typically encounter. While most youth come into care for issues that impact their family of origin, such as mental illness and substance abuse, many LGBTQ youth come into care due in large part to conflict stemming from their sexual orientation or gender identity. Therefore, traditional child welfare interventions for parents such as parenting classes, substance abuse treatment, and mental health services are likely to be much less effective than services that aim to address the specific issues that a family has related to a youth's SOGIE. Services such as intensive family counseling, psychoeducation about issues related to acceptance and rejection, as well as affirming mental health services for youth would likely be much more effective in helping to reunify LGBTQ youth with their families of origin.

Intensive family therapy has the potential to allow family members to work through the frustration, anger, and other emotions that they might experience when learning that their child is not straight or not cisgender. The support, guidance, and structure that are provided in family sessions would likely create for a much more constructive and safe environment for issues to be addressed and worked through than what many families traditionally experience when dealing with these issues on their own. These services also allow for families and youth to better deal with the high levels of emotionality that are often involved when family members may not be accepting of LGBTQ youth.

Psychoeducational services aimed at helping families and youth to better understand issues related to SOGIE would likely go a long way in easing the tension and initiating more constructive and sensitive dialogue with families. Additionally, interventions that educate family members, especially parents, on the effects of things like acceptance and rejection have proven to be very helpful in reframing how a family confronts the emotions and thoughts that they might have about their loved one's sexual orientation or gender identity. Helping families to understand that their own level of acceptance can largely impact whether or not their child will experience things like depression, suicidal thoughts, or engage in risky sexual behaviors and substance abuse is one of the most effective ways to begin to address some of the hostility and rejection that LGBTQ youth face (Ryan, Huebner, Diaz, & Sanches, 2009).

Child welfare workers often lack the training and knowledge around issues related to SOGIE that might impact families. This lack of insight tends to contribute to a workforce that doesn't seek out services that might be most appropriate in reuniting LGBTQ youth with their family of origin. Furthermore, because of the high levels of hostility, rejection, and tension that are often exhibited by families with an LGBTQ youth, child welfare professionals are much less likely to view family reunification as a viable and appropriate option. The risk and potential for further maltreatment often leads well-intended caseworkers to seek alternative permanency options for LGBTQ youth that often don't involve their families of origin. While family reunification may not be a viable and safe permanency outcome for some LGBTQ youth, this doesn't mean that child welfare professionals should not make every reasonable effort to try and reunite LGBTQ youth with their family of origin.

Many parents or caretakers are initially upset, disappointed, or angry with their child upon learning about their SOGIE; however, it is critical that child welfare professionals understand that these feelings and perceptions often change over time. Services aimed at addressing this conflict, such as therapy, education, and support, have proven to be effective in mediating conflict around issues related to youth SOGIE. Child welfare professionals who understand the important role that counseling and education can have in addressing the tension, emotionality, and hostility that many families exhibit have the potential to enhance a youth's likelihood of being reunited with their family, as well as to keep youth from more restrictive permanency options.

Placement Instability

The fact that LGBTQ youth are much less likely to be reunified with their family member means that they are more likely to enter out-of-home care. When youth enter out-of-home care, child welfare professionals are tasked with finding the least restrictive living situation available that offers the most stability for a youth. LGBTQ youth tend to experience placement instability at a much higher rate than straight youth. In fact, a study on the placement experiences of LGBTQ youth found that LGBTQ youth had an average of 6.35 placements by the time they reached permanency, a rate that is nearly double that of straight youth (Mallon, Aledort, & Ferrera, 2002). LGBTQ youth are often easy targets for bullying, harassment, and other forms of mistreatment from their peers. In many cases, caretakers such as foster parents or group home staff are not equipped to respond to these incidents of mistreatment in appropriate and affirming ways. The inadequate responses from foster parents and other caretakers that LGBTQ youth encounter create a culture in which they may not feel safe in their placements. In some cases, an LGBTQ youth may retaliate when they feel that they have been bullied or harassed. Other youth may isolate themselves as a form of protection or survival. How a youth responds to things like bullying and harassment can have a profound impact on their placement status. Behaviors such as fighting, arguing, self-harm, or isolating oneself can easily contribute to a caretaker's decision to no longer allow that youth in their home.

The hostility, rejection, and tension that many LGBTQ youth encounter in their placements can contribute to their desire to leave a placement. When an LGBTQ youth feels that they are not safe or not accepted, they may choose to seek every opportunity to sabotage their current living situation. Choosing to leave a placement where a youth feels unsafe or unwelcome can be a very complex process than can have negative consequences for a youth. Youth in out-of-home care have historically had very little voice about where they live and with whom they live. For decades, the child welfare system has experienced a critical shortage of foster parents and caregivers. Foster homes and group homes are often overcrowded, and when placement is sought for youth, especially older youth, the options are often limited. If a youth feels unwelcome or unsafe in their current placement, they typically can't simply request to be removed and placed in another home or with another family. The fact that an LGBTQ youth will likely encounter a number of obstacles when trying to leave a placement that is hostile, rejecting, or potentially dangerous often means that they have to take matters into their own hands. In such situations, a youth may act out and exhibit behaviors that might increase the chances of their removal, a term that is referred to by many child welfare professionals as placement sabotage. In other instances, a youth might run away from their placement, often to situations or settings that aren't safe.

Although it might be rare for foster parents or other caretakers to explicitly ask that an LGBTQ youth be removed because they are uncomfortable with the youth's SOGIE, some LGBTQ youth have had placements terminated due to their caregiver's refusal to allow them to remain in their placement.

Nick

Nick had a very nomadic experience in foster care before being placed with the Scott family when he was 14. In fact, Nick would convey that his first year in the Scott home was the most stable and safe that he had felt at any time in his childhood. When Nick's foster parents learned that he was gay, they informed him that this "lifestyle" was not something that aligned with the values and beliefs of their family. They went on to inform Nick that, although they loved him and felt that he was like a son to them in many ways, he could no longer live in their home if he were to continue living a gay "lifestyle". While Nick knew that he couldn't do anything to change his sexual orientation, he also knew that the Scotts provided a loving and safe home. Nick opted to do everything that he could to convince the Scott family that he was straight. He would go on dates with females from his school and be sure to share details about his romantic relationships with the Scotts. Nick would even go so far as to intentionally leave up emails that he had sent to girls noting how much he liked them. Months later, Nick's foster parents would discover that he was in a long-term relationship with a young man from his school. The news of Nick's relationship with this young man led to the Scotts making a request to have Nick removed from their care and placed into another foster home.

Maintaining placement stability has been an issue that has challenged child welfare professionals for decades. LGBTQ youth often experience placement breakdowns for reasons that have much to do with systemic flaws, and the bias, incompetence, and insensitivity of caregivers and other professionals. Unfortunately, the more placements that a youth experiences, regardless of what the reasons for the placement breakdowns might have been, the more difficult it becomes to find appropriate, long-term, placements in less restrictive environments. Once a youth compiles multiple placements, he or she is more likely to be deemed a behavioral problem and the decision for foster parents to accept them into their care is considered to come with greater risks than actually exist.

Overreliance on Congregate Care Settings

Congregate care or group home settings are typically considered to be among the least desired and most restrictive placement options for youth in out-of-home care. While it is well understood that there is necessity for congregate care placements in some situations, the consensus among child welfare professionals is that youth are best served in traditional family settings. A recent examination of the experiences of youth in congregate care found that youth in congregate care settings often encounter a number of disparities when compared to youth in more traditional care settings (Association for Children and Families, 2015). According to this study, youth in congregate care settings are nearly three times more likely to have a mental health diagnosis and over six times more likely to have been removed from a placement for behavioral reasons than youth in traditional homes. Furthermore, youth in congregate care spent an average of seven more months in care than those with no history of congregate care placement. In addition, youth who have a history of congregate care placement are significantly more likely to be involved with the juvenile justice system, as well as the adult corrections system, than those who have never been in congregate care.

LGBTQ youth are significantly more likely to end up in congregate care settings than their straight counterparts. A variety of factors contribute to the overreliance on congregate care settings for LGBTQ youth. The fact that many LGBTQ youth experience placement breakdowns for reasons that are often out of their control can lead professionals to seek placements in more restrictive settings, such as group homes and therapeutic foster homes. In many cases, an LGBTQ youth's behavioral and emotional risks do not necessitate placement in such restrictive environments. The past behaviors that many LGBTQ youth may have exhibited as a way to deal with things like rejection, hostility, and cultural incompetence may suggest that a youth needs a much greater level of supervision than what is actually necessary. Furthermore, child welfare professionals do not always closely examine the factors that may have contributed to why a placement may have broken down and the reasons why an LGBTQ youth may have felt that certain protective behaviors were appropriate or necessary. The fact that congregate care settings are often much better equipped to provide care for emotionally and behaviorally at-risk youth makes them much more convenient placement options for LGBTQ youth.

Although the consensus among child welfare professionals is that congregate care settings should be used as a last resort for most youth, this does not appear to be the case with LGBT youth. While the use of congregate care is declining for youth across the nation, some professionals question whether or not this same trend is true for LGBTQ youth. Many well-intended child welfare professionals view congregate settings as the most appropriate and least threatening option for LGBTQ youth in need of placement. The fact that there is less pressure to fit into a more traditional family setting, many child welfare professionals might view congregate care settings as being less rejecting and hostile for LGBTQ youth. Similarly, a well-intended child welfare professional might find comfort in the fact that congregate care settings are typically prone to much more oversight and regulation than traditional family foster homes and view this as a protective factor for LGBTQ youth.

Traditional family style foster homes are largely considered to be the most appropriate and least restrictive permanency options when things like family reunification, kinship placement, and adoption are not attainable. Long-term foster care with a family that is committed to caring for a youth and providing things like nurture, consistency, and normalcy may make sense for many youth. The idea of living in a family setting isn't always perceived as being an attractive option for many LGBTQ youth. The fact that so many LGBTQ youth have experienced things like rejection, hostility, and other forms of maltreatment from their families of origin they may have strong reservations about returning to a family setting. The idea of living with a family may pose the potential for further rejection, shame, and mistreatment for LGBTQ youth causing youth to be very skeptical or cautious.

Brian

When Brian's caseworker called to share the news that she had located a family that she thought would be a nice fit for him, he did not share in her excitement. Brian had established a sense of comfort and stability over the past eight months in his group home, and the idea of living with a new family at age 15 was frightening. The staff at Brian's group were very accepting and affirming, and he got along fairly well with the other kids. Unlike previous placements, the kids in this home knew that they couldn't get away with teasing and bullying him, and when they did give him a hard time, the staff were quick to intervene. While it wasn't a perfect living situation and didn't offer many of the things that he knew a really good foster home might provide in terms of things like normalcy, intimacy, and support, Brian had developed a sincere appreciation for much of what his group home offered. This is evident in the following statement from Brian:

It's like I didn't even realize how much I liked living there until my caseworker called to tell me that she found me a family. I didn't have to worry about all the shit that I usually had to worry about at other places.

Brian remembered several reasons why he was reluctant to make the transition into this foster home. While his caseworker was confident that the family would be a good fit and offer a supportive environment for Brian, he didn't know for certain if they would be accepting of him being gay. Brian had experienced other caretakers who had claimed to not have any issues with his sexual orientation but still gave him a difficult time. Brian expands on this dynamic: "When your caseworker says they found someone that's accepting that doesn't always mean what you think. Accepting for some foster parents might mean that they agree that they won't make your life a living hell and berate you because you're gay. That is not acceptance. They can still do all the little stuff that makes you feel different and like you don't belong. Or even worse, they may not even talk about it at all. I learned to be really careful when I heard that someone was accepting."

Ultimately, Brian opted to not go to the foster home, and he remained in his group home for a few more years. For Brian, the acceptance and security that he experienced in his group home outweighed the potential risk involved in not knowing how a foster family might approach issues related to his identity. Brian provides an enormous sense of insight into just how difficult this decision was for him, "I went back and forth for a long time. My caseworker was even getting impatient with me. I think if my group home could have guaranteed that I could come back if things didn't work out than I probably would have at least tried it out. Leaving a place where I didn't have to worry about being gay was just too risky. What if it didn't work out with the family and my group home filled my bed? Who knows where I would have gone? My caseworker was disappointed with me. I think my staff thought that I should go with the family, but they understood why I wanted to stay."

Thanks to the recent advocacy efforts of foster youth from around the nation, a significant amount of attention has been given to the issue of normalcy for foster youth. Foster youth and advocates have argued that youth in foster care should be provided with the same access and opportunities that many other youth have when it comes to things like sleepovers, school dances, driver's education, dating, and other extracurricular activities. While youth in traditional foster homes have faced numerous obstacles in establishing a sense of normalcy, the challenges are even greater for youth in congregate care settings.

Lack of Accepting and Affirming Families

The lack of affirming and competent foster families, in addition to the reluctance that some LGBTQ youth have toward the idea of living in a family environment, has led to an overreliance on congregate care or group home settings for LGBTQ youth. In many cases, even well-intended caseworkers perceive group care settings to be the most appropriate placement setting for LGBTQ youth. This is of concern to child welfare professionals due to the fact that congregate care settings are among the most restrictive placement options. This section will explore the challenges to finding safe and affirming foster family placements for LGBTQ youth.

Finding Accepting Foster Families

While the process of finding a foster family that is a good fit for any youth in foster care can be challenging, the process for finding families that can offer an affirming and inclusive living environment for LGBTQ youth can present some added obstacles. Factors such as low levels of compensation and increased oversight and regulation on foster homes have contributed to the critical shortage of foster parents that the US is currently facing. This critical shortage of foster parents certainly has an adverse impact on the experiences of LGBTQ youth in care. The high number of placement breakdowns that many LGBTQ youth have experienced can make foster parents very hesitant to take them into their homes. Potential foster parents who are deciding whether or not to take in a youth may not be aware of the factors related their SOGIE that may have contributed to the breakdown of placements. Similarly, the previous behaviors that an LGBTQ youth may have exhibited as a result of rejection and hostility, such as running away, retaliation in the form of aggression, or truancy, are often outside the realm of what many foster parents are comfortable with. If foster parents were aware of the unique circumstances that contribute to many of these behaviors, they might demonstrate a willingness to accept an LGBTQ youth.

While many foster parents are capable and willing to do all that they can to provide an accepting and empowering environment for LGBTQ youth, it is no secret that there are many families who are not accepting of LGBTQ youth. The fact that the pool of foster parents available to take youth is often limited, it is even smaller for foster parents who are willing and equipped to accept LGBTQ youth. The process for screening foster parents in most states does not address how a family might confront the issue of accepting an LGBTQ youth into their care. When a child welfare professional seeks out a foster placement for an LGBTQ youth, they are usually unaware of how the foster parents might feel about issues related to a youth's SOGIE. If a conversation with the foster family is not initiated at the time of the placement aimed exploring feelings related to the youth's SOGIE, there is little way of assuring that the placement is affirming and appropriate for an LGBTQ youth. Even well-intended child welfare professionals may not have the training necessary to prepare them to assess how equipped and capable a family might be to provide affirming care for an LGBTQ youth.

The process of preparing child welfare professionals to assess and identify a family's capacity to provide accepting and affirming care could go a long way in improving the experiences of LGBTQ youth. In many cases, simply asking questions exploring how comfortable the family is having an LGBTQ youth and how they might approach things like friendships, dating, and extracurricular activities can reduce the number of negative placement experiences.

Many private agencies that recruit, license, and supervise foster placements are supported through faith-based church organizations. Faith-based organizations with strong affiliations with conservative church denominations may be more likely to recruit foster families that may have religious or theological convictions that might prevent them from accepting and affirming LGBTQ youth. Efforts to recruit foster parents in more progressive communities of faith would likely help to expand the pool of foster parents who are open and equipped to caring for LGBTQ youth. Such efforts could also have a profound impact on the number of placements that LGBTQ youth experience. Placing LGBTQ youth in a family environment that offers a critical mass of nurture, acceptance, and stability early on has the potential for preventing many of the systematic challenges that many LGBTQ youth currently encounter. Issues such as frequent placement breakdowns, congregate care placements, and running away would be much less likely if a safe and supportive family that is equipped and trained to care for LGBTQ youth is an option early on.

Challenges to Recruiting Affirming and Accepting Families

While societal acceptance of LGBTQ individuals is at an all-time high, many child welfare professionals struggle with finding families who are willing to provide an accepting and affirming home for LGBTQ youth. In many states, foster families are recruited by faith-based agencies through local churches. Many families who are recruited through churches and other faith-based communities may hold theological and religious views that run counter to being accepting and affirming of LGBTQ individuals. In many cases, these families might provide excellent care to straight or cisgender youth; however, they might not be the ideal candidates to care for LGBTQ youth. While most states do not have formal screening procedures that assess a family's willingness and capacity to provide accepting and affirming care, this is certainly something that placement workers should address when placing LGBTQ youth into foster homes.

Gabe

Gabe was a child welfare professional who worked for a private agency that served children and families in a large rural area. Gabe was asked to transport a young man from an emergency shelter to a foster home in a town about 60 miles away. On the way to the foster home, Gabe was asked by the youth if it might be possible for him to continue to see his boyfriend from time to time. Gabe ensured the youth that he would ask his new foster parents if they would be willing to meet halfway from time to time so the two could see each other. When Gabe mentioned the youth's request to the foster parents at the intake meeting, both foster parents made negative comments about the youth's sexual orientation that Gabe considered offensive and insensitive. Feeling uncomfortable about placing the youth with this family, Gabe made the decision to terminate the placement arrangement and seek an alternative placement for the youth.

Kinship Care

Options to place an LGBTQ youth in kinship care may be hindered by the lack of extended family members willing to provide accepting and affirming care. When seeking out kinship care providers, child welfare professionals might overlook the fictive kinship networks that LGBTQ youth create on their own as a result of the rejection and isolation from family members. In many cases, LGBTQ youth may have teachers, coaches, parents of their peers, or other adults who have they trust and confide in. In some cases, these individuals may play a role that is very similar to that of a parent. Although these individuals may not be a part of the youth's family of origin, they are often the most trustworthy and loving adults in an LGBTQ youth's life. Efforts to seek out members of an LGBTQ youth's fictive kinship network by child welfare professionals could potentially prevent a youth from going into foster care or congregate care settings in a similar way that traditional kinship placements might.

## 5

FOSTER FAMILY ACCEPTANCE

Many individuals begin the process of becoming a foster parent without ever considering that a child or teen who moves into their home might be gay, lesbian, bisexual, transgender, or questioning. While some may have personal struggles with accepting an LGBTQ youth, many others are likely to want to create a safe and affirming home in the same way they would for straight or gender-conforming youth. Unfortunately, the process of training and preparing foster parents has historically excluded content related to a youth's sexual orientation and gender identity. Many foster parents do not have the foundational knowledge to understand what acceptance looks like and strategies for creating acceptance in the home. Similarly, many foster parents are not trained on the significance of family acceptance and the impact that it can have on the social, emotional, health, and academic well-being of LGBTQ youth.

The Importance of Acceptance

A seminal study exploring the impact that family acceptance has on the health and mental health outcomes of LGBTQ youth adults in the general population suggests that those young people with highly rejecting caregivers were nearly eight times more likely to attempt suicide, six times more likely to have depressive symptoms, three times more likely to abuse illegal drugs, and three times more likely to be at risk for HIV infection than those individuals with highly accepting caretakers (Ryan, Huebner, Diaz, & Sanches, 2009). Furthermore, this study found that LGBTQ young people with accepting caretakers were nearly three times more likely to think that they could be happy as adults than those with rejecting caretakers.

There are a number of reasons that might explain why a parent or caretaker might exhibit rejecting behaviors when their child or teenager comes out. While the research on the negative impact that family rejection can have on LGBTQ youth is clear, it is important to note that some parents may not necessarily have negative intentions when they exhibit behaviors that are often associated with rejection. Many caretakers might fear that a youth will be mistreated or marginalized by their peers or other family members and might encourage the youth to conceal or hide information about their SOGIE. Others may hold out some level of hope that the youth may be going through a phase and that over time they will identify as straight or cisgender. While these types of reactions from caretakers can certainly have profound negative consequences on a youth's health and well-being, many of these issues would likely be addressed through psychoeducation efforts aimed at helping parents to understand the impact that acceptance and rejection can have on their loved one. Understanding the negative impact that rejection has on a youth's health, mental health, and well-being and the positive ways that family acceptance can help to mediate many of the challenges and barriers that LGBTQ youth encounter is critical for families to create safe and affirming home environments for youth.

The acceptance that a youth experiences from their families or foster families can also play a pivotal role in helping them to navigate other spaces that may not be as safe and affirming, such as school or extracurricular settings. When a youth has the support of their parents, they are much more likely to seek out supportive and affirming resources such as school- and community-based programs such as gay-straight alliances (GSAs). These programs can have a profound positive impact on an LGBTQ youth's social and academic well-being (Kosciw, Greytak, Palmer, & Boesen, 2013; McCormick, Schmidt, & Clifton, 2015). Resources such as GSAs can be crucial in mediating some of the hostility and stigma that many LGBTQ youth encounter in schools. The most recent climate survey from the Gay, Lesbian, and Straight Education Network found that only 55.5% of LGBTQ teens feel safe in their current school setting. Similarly, almost one-third of LGBTQ youth missed at least one day of school in the past month for fears related to their physical safety at school.

What Does Foster Family Rejection Look Like?

Rejecting behaviors from foster parents and other caretakers can take a number of forms. In many cases, foster families may respond to an LGBTQ based upon what they know and what they've been taught around issues related to a youth's SOGIE. In some cases, foster families might have theological or religious convictions suggesting that homosexuality and gender nonconformity are in some way wrong or immoral. In many cases, when a foster parent feels that an issue related to a youth's SOGIE is sinful or wrong, they might react in ways that could potentially be harmful to the health, well-being, safety, or permanence of an LGBTQ youth. The following is a list of potentially rejecting behaviors for youth in foster care:

- Terminating an LGBTQ youth's placement for issues related to their SOGIE;
- Threatening to terminate an LGBTQ youth's placement for issues related to their SOGIE;
- Isolating LGBTQ youth from peers of the same sex;
- Pressuring LGBTQ youth to participate in gender-conforming activities;
- Refusing to discuss or acknowledge issues related to SOGIE with a youth;
- Pressuring LGBTQ youth to engage in reparative or conversion therapies;
- Blocking an LGBTQ youth's access to LGBTQ friends and allies;
- Creating double standards for LGBTQ youth with regard to romantic relationships;
- Denying LGBTQ access to resources such as GSAs, support groups, and drop-in centers;
- Allowing peers and other foster youth to harass, bully, and tease LGBTQ youth with no recourse;
- Blaming LGBTQ youth for any harassment or bullying that they receive as a result of their SOGIE;
- Expressing shame or disappointment toward an LGBTQ youth for issues related to their SOGIE;
- Suggesting to an LGBTQ youth that their SOGIE is in any way sinful, immoral, or wrong;
- Pressuring an LGBTQ youth to keep issues related to their SOGIE a secret;
- Discussing issues related to a youth's SOGIE with others (caseworkers, teachers, court advocates, etc.) without their consent.

What Does Foster Family Acceptance Look Like?

Many foster parents who may be fully accepting of an LGBTQ youth may lack the understanding and terminology related to SOGIE. Although an understanding of issues related to SOGIE is important, it is critical that professionals and caretakers do not allow a lack of understanding or terminology to prevent them from acknowledging and discussing issues related to SOGIE with youth. Additionally, it is essential that caretakers and child welfare professionals know what acceptance in the context of foster care looks like and routinely assess the ways in which they can enhance acceptance and affirmation for LGBTQ youth. The following is a list of potentially accepting behaviors for youth in foster care:

- Acknowledging a youth's SOGIE and openly discussing their identity,
- Ensuring that all youth and adults in the home respect an LGBTQ youth,
- Creating zero-tolerance policies for harassment, teasing, and bullying for issues related to a youth's SOGIE,
- Understanding that not all challenges and struggles that an LGBTQ youth encounters are a result of their SOGIE,
- Encouraging LGBTQ youth to participate in activities and hobbies that they are passionate about,
- Using inclusive language that respect a youth's preference in pronouns,
- Connecting youth with LGBTQ peers and allies that embrace their SOGIE,
- Advocating for LGBTQ youth when they are mistreated or bullied,
- Ensuring that LGBTQ youth have similar rules when it comes to romantic relationships and dating,

- Recognizing that you don't have to choose between your moral or religious values and providing a loving and accepting home for an LGBTQ youth, and
- Understanding that LGBTQ youth can be happy with their LGBTQ identity.

Understanding the Role of Acceptance in the Lives of LGBTQ Youth in Care

A recent study aimed at comparing the experiences of LGBTQ in accepting foster families to those in rejecting families suggests that foster family acceptance can play a critical role in mediating many of the challenges and barriers that LGBTQ youth encounter as they navigate the child welfare system (McCormick, Schmidt, & Terrazas, 2016). Accepting experiences in foster care can have an especially profound impact on enriching and encouraging discussions around a youth's SOGIE, eliminating double standards, and enhancing a youth's sense of stability and permanence.

ACKNOWLEDGEMENT

LGBTQ youth in foster families that they consider to be accepting often express that their caretakers were much better equipped and willing to discuss issues related to their SOGIE. These conversations are often instrumental in serving as pathways to conversations about other topics that youth consider intimate or sensitive. For many youth, the fact that their foster parents are willing and open to engaging in a dialogue about issues related to their SOGIE suggests that they are likely a safe and trustworthy individual to confide in about other sensitive issues.

Many youth with accepting foster family experiences credit their foster parents for helping them to navigate conversations related to their SOGIE with other adults and professionals. For many LGBTQ youth, the safety and affirmation that they experience from their foster parents empowers them to engage in similar conversations with caseworkers, advocates, lawyers, and other adults involved in their lives. Youth note that, in many cases, they feel a sense of comfort in discussing these issues knowing that even if they don't get the reaction or response that they desire from others, their foster parents will be there to provide support.

The systemic and structural barriers that many LGBTQ youth encounter in the child welfare system often force them to conceal or hide information about their SOGIE. In addition, many LGBTQ youth are in care for reasons that pertain to the hostility or rejection that they experienced from their families. When a foster family creates a space in which a youth no longer has to try and hide or conceal their SOGIE, they are much more likely to be empowered in other ways.

While youth in homes that are accepting are likely to experience a sense of empowerment and liberation around the acknowledgement and safety they have around discussions related to their SOGIE, youth in rejecting foster homes have a much different experience. The dialogue that serves as the catalyst for discussion on other sensitive or intimate topics for youth in accepting homes is often non-existent for youth in rejecting homes. In many cases, LGBTQ youth perceive a caretaker's unwillingness to acknowledge or discuss issues related to their SOGIE as a barrier to initiating conversations about other sensitive topics. It makes sense that a youth might not have the confidence or comfort in their caretakers to have an affirming or appropriate reaction to other issues even if they have little or nothing to do with their SOGIE. Furthermore, a foster parent's lack of willingness and comfort in discussing sensitive issues related to SOGIE sends a message to youth that others might be equally as unsafe or unwilling to discuss issues with. In response to this silence, a youth might be more likely to isolate and internalize any feelings or experiences that they have related to their SOGIE. The silence that an LGBTQ youth experiences can also be perceived as shame or disappointment.

RESPONSES TO MISTREATMENT

The responses that a foster parent has to the mistreatment, bullying, or harassment that an LGBTQ youth experiences can profoundly impact their relationship with the youth. Given the fact that LGBTQ youth in foster care often have to deal with the stigma of being in foster care, as well as the stigma related to their SOGIE, it's essential that foster families respond appropriately to any mistreatment. Youth with accepting foster families are likely to perceive their foster families as advocates and allies if and when they experience mistreatment. For many, their foster parents go to great lengths to ensure that they are treated no differently than other youth. Accepting foster parents ensure that youth do not encounter double standards in school, church, or other settings and are willing to speak up for the rights and respect of youth in their care. In addition, accepting families are certain to be sensitive to the fact that not all of the problems or challenges that an LGBTQ youth experiences are a direct result of issues related to their SOGIE.

For youth with rejecting foster families, the responses that they experience to mistreatment like bullying and harassment often look much different. In many cases, they are blamed for the mistreatment and instructed or encouraged to not discuss issues related to their SOGIE to prevent future encounters.

Double Standards

Perhaps one of the most important things that families can do to foster acceptance and affirmation for LGBTQ youth is to avoid the use of double standards in their homes. LGBTQ youth in accepting homes note the great lengths that their foster parents went to in attempts to level the playing field when it comes to things like access to LGBTQ peers and allies, romantic relationships, and extracurricular activities. Given the multitude of disparities that LGBTQ youth in care experience when compared to straight and cisgender youth, efforts to enhance fairness and equality can go a long way for LGBTQ youth in care.

For many youth, access to friends and romantic partners is often forbidden or discouraged. In many cases, LGBTQ youth are prevented from pursuing romantic relationships, while their straight peers are encouraged or, at the very least, allowed to engage in age-appropriate romantic relationships. It is essential that LGBTQ youth have the same access to privileges and opportunities both in and out of their foster homes that straight and cisgender youth have.

A similar dynamic often exists when it comes to access to other LGBTQ youth or allies. Youth in accepting families are much more likely to report that their foster parents assist them in seeking out friendships and support. In some cases, youth were encouraged to join GSAs and other groups. LGBTQ youth in rejecting families are often discouraged and even prohibited from engaging in friendships with other LGBTQ youth and straight allies.

Youth express that, in some cases, their foster parents feel that these relationships and friendships will only serve to enable youth to identify in a way that they deem inappropriate.

The Ideal Foster Family

When asked to describe the ideal foster family, LGBTQ youth in both accepting and rejecting families clearly feel as though acceptance and affirmation are the most important qualities to possess. A common theme among LGBTQ youth in accepting families is their willingness to overlook the potential shortcomings of families if the family is simply willing to be accepting of their SOGIE. This dynamic is strongly emphasized in the following quote from Liz, a former foster youth who lived with an accepting family for two years before aging out of care: "I didn't care if they were too strict or that they did other things that drove me crazy. They accepted that I was gay and I knew that I wasn't going to do anything to mess this placement up".

In addition to acceptance, youth often identify communication and acknowledgement as other qualities that are essential in an accepting foster family. LGBTQ youth are likely to stress the significance of creating a culture in the home where there are dialogues and discussions around issues related to SOGIE. Many LGBTQ youth fear that their foster parent's lack of understanding or confidence about issues related to SOGIE will serve as a barrier to having an open and thoughtful discussion. Although a comprehensive understanding of issues and terminology related to a youth's SOGIE is important, it is critical that foster parents not avoid these conversations due to their own lack of confidence or comfort. Without knowing where their foster parents might stand on certain issues, LGBTQ youth are likely to assume the worst, a pattern that will only create more distance and silence in their relationship.

Findings from studies on foster family acceptance can prove to be very important in helping to create a culture of acceptance and affirmation for LGBTQ youth. Efforts to train and educate foster families on the potential impact that acceptance can have on the lives of LGBTQ youth can likely go a long way in helping foster parents to recognize the importance of responding in appropriate, supportive, and proactive ways. Furthermore, training efforts are essential in helping foster families to gain the confidence and understanding necessary to engage in conversations that are sensitive and empowering.

6

TRAUMA-INFORMED CARE AND LGBTQ YOUTH IN CARE

Societal acceptance of LGBTQ youth has increased significantly over the past decade. Far more youth than ever before self-identify as LGBTQ, and the age in which youth "come out" is steadily dropping (Shilo & Savaya, 2011). Another significant development that has taken place over the course of the past decade has been the growth and popularity of trauma-informed care. The field of trauma assessment and treatment for children and youth has experienced unprecedented gains and improvements over the past decade. Systems, such as the child welfare system, that are responsible for responding to the traumatic stress experienced by children and families are much better equipped to respond in sensitive and informed ways thanks to the increased knowledge and emphasis placed on trauma-informed care. Despite the fact that the advances in trauma-informed responses to children and families have largely occurred during the same period of time that LGBTQ youth have experienced more acceptance than ever before, LGBTQ youth have largely been excluded from conversations on trauma-informed care.

LGBTQ youth experience nearly every form of trauma and maltreatment at disproportionately high rates. The stigma and marginalization that many LGBTQ youth experience makes them especially vulnerable to trauma and traumatic stress. This increased vulnerability provides further evidence of the need for trauma-informed interventions that specifically address issues related to a youth's SOGIE.

Increased Vulnerability to Traumatic Stress for LGBTQ Youth

The fact that LGBTQ youth experience multiple forms of trauma and maltreatment at significantly higher rates than straight and cisgender youth suggests that they are often more likely to develop traumatic stress. In fact, a recent study exploring the rates of posttraumatic stress disorder (PTSD) in sexual minority youth suggests that LGBTQ youth are nearly 3.9 times more likely to experience PTSD than straight or cisgender youth (Roberts, Rosario, Corliss, Koenen, & Austin, 2012a). This same study found that nearly 9% of young adult men and 20% of women with sexual minority identities have a lifetime risk of PTSD. Many of these individuals reported victimization experiences during their childhood. Just over 45% of sexual minority women and 28% of sexual minority men report having some childhood victimization experience. This can be compared to the childhood victimization rates for straight or cisgender men (20%) and women (21%).

Children who exhibit gender nonconformity are among the most vulnerable populations when it comes to childhood victimization. A recent study exploring the relationship between childhood gender nonconformity and victimization suggests that gender nonconforming boys are nearly three times more likely to experience sexual abuse during their childhood than cisgender boys (Roberts, Rosario, Corliss, Koenen, & Austin, 2012b). Similarly, nonconforming girls are almost 60% more likely to have experience victimization during their childhood than cisgender girls.

School Victimization

In addition to the increased levels of vulnerability that LGBTQ youth experience in their homes and communities, they are often more vulnerable to victimization in their schools. In the most recent climate study on LGBTQ youth in schools, 55.5% of LGBTQ youth reported that felt unsafe in their school for reasons pertaining to their SOGIE (Kosciw, Greytak, Palmer, & Boesen, 2013). Missing school, dropping out, and truancy have often been significant problems for many LGBTQ youth. Nearly a third of LGBTQ (30%) youth in the climate study missed at least one day of school in the last month for fears for their safety. An even larger percentage (35.4%) reported that they routinely avoid gender-segregated spaces for fear that they may be victimized. A similar percentage of LGBTQ youth (36.3%) have experienced some form of physical harassment at school during the past year. When these same youth were surveyed about physical assault experiences, a staggering 16.5% had been physically assaulted on school grounds.

What's equally as alarming is that most LGBTQ youth do not report their victimization experiences to teachers and administrators. Just over half of those students who were physically assaulted at school made no report to school officials for fears that they would not intervene effectively and make things even worse for the youth (Kosciw et al., 2013). Of those youth who did report, 61% suggest that the school personnel engaged in no action in response to the report.

In addition to their increased vulnerability to victimization experiences in schools, LGBTQ youth are often much more vulnerable to microaggressions from their peers and, in some cases, faculty and staff. An overwhelming percentage (85%) of LGBTQ youth were verbally harassed at school, and 65% were frequently referred to with homophobic terms, such as "fag" or "dyke".

Dating Violence

Perhaps one of the forms of victimization that LGBTQ youth experience at disproportionately high rates is dating violence. A recent study on the dating violence experiences of LGBTQ suggests that nearly a quarter (23%) of LGBTQ youth report at least one experience of sexual dating violence as compared to 9% of straight youth (CDC, 2011). Similarly, the percentage of lesbian and gay youth who report experiences of physical dating violence (42.8%) is significantly higher than that of straight youth (29%). Transgender youth are among the most vulnerable populations to experience dating violence with 88% of transgender youth having at least one experience of dating violence before the age of 18 (Dank, Lachman, Yahner, & Zweig, 2014).

Risky Behaviors among LGBTQ Youth

It's no secret that LGBTQ youth have historically and continue to engage in many risky behaviors than straight and cisgender youth (Centers for Disease Control, 2011; Marshal et al., 2008; Ryan, Huebner, Diaz, & Sanches, 2009). In fact, the risky behaviors exhibited by LGBTQ youth are perhaps the area of research that has gotten the most attention. It has been well known for a long time that LGBTQ youth use and abuse substances at rates much higher than straight youth. In fact, recent studies suggest that LGBTQ youth are nearly three times more likely to abuse illegal substances than straight youth (Marshal et al., 2008). The risky sexual behaviors that LGBTQ youth engage in have also been well documented. According to the Centers for Disease Control (2011), LGBTQ youth have intercourse before the age of 13 at a rate that is nearly four times higher than straight youth (19.8% vs. 4.8%). In addition, LGBTQ youth report having significantly more sexual partners than straight youth. Nearly a third (29%) of LGBTQ youth have had at least four sexual partners, a rate percentage that is nearly three times higher than that of straight youth (11%). LGBTQ youth are also much less likely to use condoms during sexual intercourse than straight youth (35% vs. 65%).

LGBTQ youth are also much more likely to engage in survival sex or to be trafficked for sex. Research suggests that LGBTQ young people who engage in same-sex sexual activity are more likely to have traded sex for things like money, residence, or food than straight or cisgender youth (Garofalo, Deleon, Osmer, Doll, & Harper, 2006). Societal homophobia, biphobia, and transphobia may have ways of pushing LGBTQ youth toward the sex trade for various reasons. Just under half of the transgender women report participating in the sex trade as a result of failure to find other forms of employment due to negative responses to their gender identity (Wilson & Widom, 2010). In some cases, LGBTQ young people report experiencing commercial sex as a way to receive affirmation of their SOGIE and to live their sexuality and gender openly (Lutnick, 2016).

A recent study on the experiences of LGBTQ youth who were engaged in survival sex suggests that most youth who were surveyed were either kicked out of their homes or were forced to flee violent or hostile home environments (Dank, Lachman, Yahner, & Zweig, 2015). This same study suggests that LGBTQ youth who engage in survival sex, including sex for pay, food, and/or residence, report that this practice often leads to very risky and dangerous circumstances. In many cases, LGBTQ youth who are engaged in survival sex are much more vulnerable to physical and sexual violence, exploitation, and human trafficking (Dank et al., 2015).

Suicide and Self-Harm

The risks associated with suicide among LGBTQ youth have been well documented in recent years (Haas, Rodgers, & Herman, 2014; Liu & Mustanki, 2012). Several high-profile cases have shed some light on the struggles and challenges that might contribute to an LGBTQ youth's suicidal ideations and attempts. LGBTQ youth are significantly more likely to both consider and attempt suicide, and the measures they take are oftentimes much more severe. LGBTQ youth are between two and seven times more likely to make a suicidal attempt than straight and cisgender youth (Haas et al., 2014). Nearly half of transgender youth reported having recently contemplated suicide (Grossman & D'Augelli, 2007). Among transgender youth adults, roughly 40% had made a suicidal attempt at least once in their lifetime (Haas et al., 2014).

While it is important to recognize the disparities in terms of the prevalence of suicide and suicidal ideations between LGBTQ youth and straight or cisgender youth, it's equally as important to understand the severity of intensity of those ideations and attempts. LGBTQ youth who make an attempt at suicide are significantly more likely to report that they had truly hoped the attempt would end their life. Similarly, LGBTQ youth are much more likely to use more lethal methods when attempting to suicide, such as using a firearm or suffocation.

Non-suicidal self-harm has become a major public health concern for LGBTQ youth in recent years. Nearly half of

LGBTQ youth report having engaged in some form of non-suicidal self-harming behavior, with the most common form being cutting on one's arms or legs (Liu & Mustanski, 2012). Previous victimization experiences have routinely been identified as one of the strongest risk factors associated with self-harming behaviors among LGBTQ youth. In addition to previous victimization experiences, other risk factors associated with self-harm among LGBTQ youth were perceived feelings of hopelessness, low levels of social support, and sensation-seeking behaviors (Liu & Mustanski, 2012).

A Conceptual Framework for Understanding Traumatic Stress Responses in LGBTQ Youth in Foster Care

The following section will utilize the Core Concepts of Understanding Traumatic Stress Responses developed by the National Child Traumatic Stress Network to develop a framework for better understanding the risky behaviors exhibited by some LGBTQ youth in care (NCTSN, 2012). In addition, this framework will use the Core Concepts to explore practice and policy responses that are sensitive to the unique risks and resilience of LGBTQ youth.

Child welfare researchers and practitioners have typically looked to factors such as family rejection, stigma, and discrimination when attempting to explain the high rates of risky behaviors exhibited by LGBTQ youth. While research has certainly shown a strong association between these factors and risky behaviors among LGBTQ youth, far less attention has been given to the potential ways in which a youth's response to traumatic stress might be contributing to their risky behaviors. The recent insights and developments in the areas of trauma-informed care have the potential to be instrumental in understanding both the risk and resilience of LGBTQ youth in care.

Secondary Adversities and LGBTQ Youth

Trauma-informed frameworks stress the importance of the secondary adversities and changes that children and youth often experience in the aftermath of traumatic experiences. Traumatic experiences are often accompanied by secondary adversities such as family separation, financial hardships, removal from parents, new school placements, social stigma, and many other potential adversities. The secondary adversities that many LGBTQ youth experience in the aftermath of trauma and maltreatment can be especially complex. When LGBTQ youth are placed in care, they are routinely faced with the challenge of assessing whether or not they are physically and emotionally safe to come out to new caretakers, caseworkers, and peers. Once in care, LGBTQ youth are much more vulnerable to added forms of maltreatment. Professionals must be able to effectively recognize and intervene to ensure that LGBTQ youth understand that these are secondary adversities that have resulted from the trauma, neglect, and/or maltreatment that they initially came into care for. When secondary adversities are not adequately addressed, they can easily be internalized by LGBTQ youth as something that they might be responsible or at fault for.

Posttraumatic Adversities and Risky Behaviors in LGBTQ Youth

Researchers, caretakers, and child welfare professionals are understandably quick to look at issues of rejection, prejudice, and stigma in explaining the reasons behind why LGBTQ youth might engage in risky behaviors such as substance abuse, truancy, and risky sexual activity. While these factors are certainly strong predictors of risky behaviors, issues related to trauma and the ways in which LGBTQ youth respond to traumatic stress can easily be overlooked and underestimated. Exposure to traumatic experiences such as physical abuse, sexual abuse, and other forms of violence can adversely affect LGBTQ youth in a number of ways. The thoughts and emotions that youth are flooded with when they encounter a traumatic reminder can contribute to behaviors that are risky, regressive, and dangerous. It is important that professionals and caretakers be sensitive to the fact that the behaviors exhibited by LGBTQ youth in care are often an attempt to respond internally to the overwhelming emotions of fear, anger, and sadness that they re-experience when triggered.

Danger and Safety in the Lives of LGBTQ Youth

Traumatic stress routinely puts youth in situations in which their sense of safety is threatened. In response, a youth will have a heightened level of concern and interest in the safety and threat of their immediate environment. The process of restoring a youth's sense of safety and security requires that practitioners are sensitive to the unique needs of LGBTQ youth, as well as the systemic and environmental responses to meeting those needs. While traumatic experiences can impact a youth's capacity to distinguish between safe and unsafe situations, such assessments can be especially challenging for LGBTQ youth (NCTSN, 2012). LGBTQ youth often have added assessments to make in determining whether a helping professional or foster parent will be a source of safety or a source of fear and concern. LGBTQ youth are often scanning their environment for indications that would help them to assess the safety of certain people and situations. Professionals and caretakers who are intentional about displaying signs and other symbols that convey that they are safe and accepting of LGBTQ individuals can help to alleviate these concerns. In addition, practitioners who make efforts to use inclusive language that is sensitive to pronouns and other terminology can be influential in conveying to youth that they are safe and supportive.

LGBTQ youth in care are often placed in environments in which stressors and potential trauma reminders are very prevalent. Studies assessing the experiences of LGBTQ youth in care clearly portray the reality that many live and navigate very unsafe and threatening environments. Practitioners and caretakers must be equipped to identify and eliminate as many of those stressors and traumatic reminders as possible in their attempt to create a sense of safety and comfort.

Public and private child welfare agencies and programs can help to enhance safety and reduce threats to LGBTQ youth by adopting nondiscrimination policies that are explicit in including provisions and language related to a youth's SOGIE. These policies, whenever possible, should cover caretakers, employees, contractors, and partner organizations. Another effective measure that agencies can take in their attempts to address safety for LGBTQ is to adopt zero-tolerance policies when it comes to youth homophobic, bi-phobic, and transphobic language and behaviors. Youth and staff should be made keenly aware of the fact that derogatory language is not tolerated in foster homes, groups, homes, offices, and any other settings. Furthermore, whistle-blower policies that protect staff and youth who do speak up when they witness mistreatment of LGBTQ youth should be clearly articulated to protect those who come forward to report harassment or mistreatment.

LGBTQ youth in care are likely to encounter a number of stressors and triggers that relate to their SOGIE. The impact of overt homophobia, biphobia, and transphobia has been documented here already, yet it is much subtler forms of rejection or microaggressions that are likely more pervasive and, if not immediately, then collectively as traumatizing. It is critical that professionals and caretakers take into consideration the interactions that LGBTQ youth have beyond the scope of the services being provided, in the context of family, school, community, media, and the society at large. Through coordinated school and family interventions, practitioners and systems can often mitigate the harmful effects of these repeated rejections.

Trauma-informed care stresses the importance of efforts that improve the level of functioning and sensitivity of a youth's support system. For LGBTQ youth in the child welfare system, their support and family system might look much different from that of other youth. The hostility and rejection that they experience from their families of origin can prevent child welfare professionals from working with families to enhance their understanding and sensitivity toward issues related to their youth's SOGIE. In some cases, even those practitioners who are willing to work with a family in an attempt to strengthen their levels of acceptance often lack the skills, theoretical knowledge, and experience around issues related to SOGIE.

Trauma-informed efforts addressing the immediate environment of LGBTQ youth must address the manner in which issues such as rejection, hostility, and tension might be contributing to the adverse effects of trauma and traumatic stress. Furthermore, professionals must understand that their attempts at recognizing trauma reminders and environmental stressors, which often involve a youth's family, may be undermined in situations where tension, rejection, and hostility are present. Trauma-informed practitioners and caretakers must have the capacity to effectively assess the complex dynamics that might exist in families of LGBTQ youth. Practitioners with the skills and knowledge base needed to address the impact that issues related to a youth' SOGIE can have on a youth's immediate environment are much more likely to create emotional and physical safety for LGBTQ youth. In addition, a youth's family of origin and/or foster family will likely be more open to acceptance and affirmation if they are aware of the impact that rejection and hostility can potentially have on an LGBTQ youth.

Discussion

One of the distinct features of trauma-informed care is the emphasis that is placed on the ways in which cultural issues can influence the manner in which youth and families respond to traumatic events (NCTSN, 2012). While cultural factors related to SOGIE may have not always been at the forefront of conversations about trauma-informed care, there is no question these factors are critical in the formulation of trauma-informed approaches for LGBTQ youth. In many cases, a youth's SOGIE can make them much more vulnerable to multiple forms of trauma. A trauma-informed framework that seeks to specifically address the environmental factors that contribute to such disproportionately high rates of traumatic exposure in LGBTQ youth is critical. In the same ways that the trauma experiences of LGBTQ youth might look a little different in many cases than those of youth who are straight or cisgender, the needs of LGBTQ youth who are responding to traumatic stress might be unique in some ways. Since LGBTQ youth are more vulnerable to traumatic experiences, it could easily be argued that a youth's SOGIE can make them more vulnerable to the adverse effects of traumatic stress. A trauma-informed framework is essential in addressing many of those vulnerabilities by assessing the ways in which a youth's SOGIE might adversely impact the intrinsic and extrinsic capacities that are critical in responding to traumatic stress.

The impact that factors such as family rejection, marginalization, and bullying can have on LGBTQ youth can present some challenges for trauma-informed practitioners and child welfare professionals. In many cases, the responses that a youth might have to such factors look a lot like the stress responses that often occur in the aftermath of a traumatic experience. The risky behaviors that an LGBTQ youth who is dealing with family or peer rejection often exhibit, such as substance abuse, truancy, self-harm, and risky sexual behaviors, are very similar to the regressive and risky behaviors that often result from traumatic stress responses. Trauma-informed approaches must seek to better prepare child welfare professionals and caretakers to make such distinctions and ensure that an LGBTQ youth's experiences with trauma are not being overlooked or de-emphasized.

The fact that LGBTQ youth are much more vulnerable to trauma and experience significant disparities related to health, mental health, and education outcomes makes it very easy for child welfare professionals and policy makers to emphasize the risks associated with LGBTQ youth in care. While trauma-informed efforts must take into account the numerous risks that are associated with LGBGQ youth, it is important that the resilience and resourcefulness of LGBTQ youth is not overlooked or underestimated. Despite the numerous barriers, obstacles, and disparities that exist for many LGBTQ youth, this is a population with far more resilience than risk. While this resilience and resourcefulness might take a form that looks different in many cases than that of youth who are straight and/or cisgender, it is essential that practitioners be equipped to assess and incorporate the strengths and resources of LGBTQ youth.

7

RECOMMENDATIONS FOR PRACTICE

The child welfare system's failure to acknowledge and address issues related to youth SOGIE has contributed to a number of challenges and disparities for LGBTQ youth. The fact that the system has been in its response to the needs of LGBTQ youth suggests that practice and policy measures can have a profound impact when it comes to creating a more inclusive and responsive system of care for LGBTQ youth. In some cases, even small measures from child welfare professionals and caretakers can go a long way in creating a sense of safety and normalcy for LGBTQ youth.

Recommendations for Child Welfare Professionals

Recognize That Perceptions, Attitudes, and Beliefs about LGBTQ Youth Can Change

As societal acceptance of LGBTQ youth increases, individuals are becoming much more knowledgeable about issues related to SOGIE. Psychoeducation specifically aimed at helping families to recognize the role that their acceptance and affirmation can have on an LGBTQ youth's health, happiness, and well-being can go a long way in fostering acceptance and understanding. Parents and foster parents who are equipped with the knowledge and insight that they can play a critical role in reducing an LGBTQ youth's likelihood of attempting suicide, being depressed, or engaging in risky sex or substance abuse are likely going to be much more open to fostering a culture of acceptance.

Child welfare professionals can help to equip families and foster families with the knowledge and insight about family acceptance through trainings and conversations. Even slight increases in a family's level of acceptance can profoundly improve the health and well-being of LGBTQ youth in care.

Acknowledge and Discuss Issues Related to SOGIE with Youth and Families

The lack of acknowledgement of LGBTQ youth in the child welfare system has proved to be one of the greatest barriers to creating a more inclusive and affirming system of care. Child welfare professionals must be aware of the dynamics that contribute to the disproportionate overrepresentation of LGBTQ youth in the system and recognize the likelihood that they will work with multiple LGBTQ youth over time. Simply acknowledging the presence of LGBTQ youth can help child welfare professionals to be much more sensitive in their approach to working with youth and their families.

Child welfare professionals must develop a sense of comfort and willingness to openly discuss issues related to a youth's SOGIE. Education and training on the most up-to-date terminology and developments on issues and topics related to a youth's SOGIE can profoundly improve a child welfare professional's competence and confidence in initiating dialogue and addressing things like stigma and discrimination. LGBTQ youth can experience a sense of liberation and empowerment when they do not have to hide or mask their feelings, thoughts, and experiences related to their SOGIE.

*Help Youth and Families to Develop the Inner Strength to
Deal with Hostility and Discrimination*

Well-intended child welfare professionals and caretakers
might feel that it's in an LGBTQ youth's best interest to
remain in the closet and not share critical information
related to their SOGIE. While in some cases an LGBTQ
youth's peers can be so rejecting or hostile that this approach might seem appropriate, in many cases, however,
an LGBTQ youth will be happier and healthier after
coming out to their families, friends, or foster families.
It is important that child welfare professionals have the
skills and capacity to help LGBTQ youth to adequately
weigh the pros and cons of coming out. There are many
benefits to coming out that are often overlooked or
underestimated by well-intended adults, as well as by
LGBTQ youth. Many of the positive benefits of coming
out include:

- Living a more authentic and whole life,
- Developing closer and more genuine relationships,
- Developing self-esteem for being known and loved for
  who you really are,
- Reducing the stress and fear of hiding who you are
  from others,
- Having open and authentic friendship and relation-
  ships with other LGBTQ youth,
- Becoming a role model for other LGBTQ youth, and
- Improved performance and attendance in school.

The potential benefits of coming out should be explored
and processed in ways that allow an LGBTQ youth to consider things that they may have not considered on their own.
In addition, child welfare professionals should be equally as

equipped to explore and discuss some of the potential risks associated with coming out. Some of the potential risks that should be explored include:

- Not everyone will be accepting or understanding;
- Some family, friends, or foster parents will be shocked, disappointed, or even hostile;
- Bullying may begin or worsen;
- Some relationships may permanently change; and
- Parents or foster parents may no longer allow youth to remain in their homes.

It is important to understand that coming out is never a one-time event for an LGBTQ youth. The decision for LGBTQ youth in foster care to come out to certain adults or peers can be especially complex considering that they often have multiple individuals involved in their lives and permanency situations. When an LGBTQ youth comes out or shares sensitive information about their SOGIE, child welfare professionals should be especially sensitive to issues of confidentiality and privacy. Child welfare professionals should never share information about a youth's SOGIE with colleagues or caregivers without getting consent from the youth.

When a youth does come out to child welfare professionals, it is important that professionals recognize the courage and resilience that often accompany a youth's decision to come out. Child welfare professionals can consider doing any combination of the following in the event that a youth has come out or shared sensitive information about their SOGIE:

- Thank them for conveying a sense of trust and confidence and explore where that trust and confidence come from,

- Acknowledge the courage and resilience that a youth has displayed by coming out and explore where that courage and resilience come from,
- Begin to explore additional resources or sources of support that a youth might want to consider,
- Weigh the potential pros and cons of coming out to others when necessary,
- Ask about relationships or current romantic partners that the youth may wish to talk about,
- Ensure that the information that was confided in you will remain confidential and private, and
- Let them know that they are supported and you will do everything you can to ensure that others are supportive.

Recognize That Not All Challenges and Adversities That LGBTQ Youth Experience Are Related to Their SOGIE

While LGBTQ youth are more vulnerable to bullying, harassment, and marginalization, it is important for child welfare professionals to understand that LGBTQ youth may encounter adversity and struggles for reasons that have little or nothing to do with their SOGIE. In an effort to ensure that LGBTQ youth are not defined by their SOGIE, child welfare professionals should be careful not to assume that all of an LGBTQ youth's adversities are a result of mistreatment or insensitivity related to their SOGIE. Adversities such as mental illness, substance use, or risky behaviors are often a part of youth's development, and, in some cases, they may have nothing to do with a youth's SOGIE.

Display Signs, Banners, or Other Safe Space Symbols

The negative experiences that LGBTQ youth have had with other adults, peers, family members, and even helping professionals will often color their interactions with child welfare professionals. LGBTQ youth are often scanning their environment to look for signs that child welfare professionals are safe and supportive of issues that relate to their SOGIE. By displaying signs, banners, or other markers that convey safety and acceptance, child welfare workers can keep LGBTQ youth from having to assume, guess, or figure out on their own whether or not they can be honest and open about their SOGIE. Safe space symbols can contribute to a much more inclusive environment where youth are more open and safe in discussing issues that relate to their SOGIE. In addition, LGBTQ youth might be open to discussing other sensitive or intimate issues when they feel a sense of safety and affirmation. Many child welfare workers meet with youth in their homes or at settings outside of their offices. In some cases, child welfare professionals might consider wearing a pin or putting a sticker on their phone, notebook, clipboard, or other items that will be in plain sight of youth.

Recognize That Previous Experiences with Helping Professionals May Color the Interactions of LGBTQ Youth

The interactions that LGBTQ youth have with other adults and helping professionals can profoundly impact their initial perceptions and interactions with child welfare professionals. In some cases, LGBTQ youth may be holding out for signs or cues that professionals are safe or supportive. Similarly, the previous negative experiences with others might impact an LGBTQ youth's initial willingness to open up or confide in child welfare workers. In such instances, it is important that child welfare professionals be sensitive and patient with youth. In addition, efforts that seek to explore or assess how LGBTQ youth feel about previous professionals they've worked with can be a very constructive and competent way to build trust and rapport.

In instances where youth have had negative experiences with other who were in helping roles, a child welfare professional might consider collaborating with LGBTQ youth to identify ways that they can be affirming and sensitive to issues related to a youth's SOGIE. When working with LGBTQ youth who have had previous negative experiences with professionals, some areas that child welfare professionals might want to consider when exploring include:

- Qualities and characteristics that LGBTQ youth value most in helping professionals,
- The ways in which previous encounters have impacted the feelings and thoughts that LGBTQ youth have about themselves, and
- The specific behaviors and reactions of previous professionals that kept LGBTQ youth from discussing issues related to their SOGIE.

Think Creatively about Social Support Networks and Fictive Kinship Networks

In response to the rejection and isolation that many LGBTQ youth in care have experienced from their families of origin, many LGBTQ youth rely heavily upon peers, mentors, and other adults to broaden their support networks, create a sense of community, and enhance some level of social control in their lives. The support networks of LGBTQ youth might look much different from the support or kinship networks of other youth in care. Child welfare professionals may consider exploring the people and relationships that an LGBTQ youth value and rely upon most. In some cases, teachers, mentors, the parents of peers, or other adults may provide many of the resources that family members would traditionally provide.

In instances where LGBTQ youth have little relational involvement with their families, they might rely more heavily on their peers for support, intimacy, and community. The size and quality of an LGBTQ youth's support network can have a profound impact on their experiences in care, and child welfare professionals can enhance and strengthen those support networks by working with youth to identify the individuals they trust and rely upon most.

Recognize That LGBTQ Youth Are Especially Vulnerable to Trauma and Traumatic Stress Responses

LGBTQ youth experience nearly all forms of trauma at disproportionately high rates. Given the high rates of exposure to traumatic experiences such as physical abuse, sexual abuse, and other forms of violence, LGBTQ youth are much more likely to experience traumatic stress. The effects of the rejection and hostility that many LGBTQ youth experience from their families and other caregivers and professionals are often the focus of child welfare professionals. It is important that the traumatic experiences and traumatic stress responses not be overlooked or minimized when assessing the behaviors, thoughts, and emotions of LGBTQ youth. Child welfare professionals should be especially aware of the role that traumatic stress might have in the risky behaviors, such as substance abuse and risky sexual activities. In many cases, these behaviors are a direct response to the overwhelming emotions, thoughts, and memories associated with traumatic experiences.

Child welfare professionals should pay careful attention to issues of fear and danger when working with LGBTQ youth in the aftermath of a traumatic experience. Checking in to assess issues related to threat and ensure that LGBTQ youth feel safe in their placement settings can go a long way in strengthening the trauma-informed response of child welfare professionals.

Recognize That LGBTQ Youth May Be Reluctant to Living in Family Settings

Given the negative and hostile experiences that many LGBTQ youth have had with their families of origin, some LGBTQ youth may be hesitant or even opposed to living in family settings. The idea of living with a traditional foster family or adoptive family may elicit feelings of betrayal and rejection. Some LGBTQ youth may fear that dynamics similar to what they experienced with their families may exist to some extent in the context of a foster family. Child welfare professionals should seek to address these issues directly with youth and make every effort to find families that are affirming and accepting of a youth's SOGIE. By processing and discussing an LGBTQ youth's fears and concerns about living in a family setting, child welfare professionals can better identify the qualities and characteristics that might be most beneficial in a potential foster family. Child welfare professionals should not rely on congregate care or group home settings for LGBTQ youth. By relying heavily on congregate care and group home settings, child welfare professionals reinforce the idea that an LGBTQ youth is not suitable or worthy of an accepting family.

When placing LGBTQ youth with foster families, child welfare professionals should consider exploring some of the ways in which the youth's previous family experiences might color their interactions with a foster family. Foster families should be encouraged to be patient and sensitive to the fact that an LGBTQ youth might have some reservations or concerns about returning to a family environment.

Allow LGBTQ Youth to Have a Voice in Major Permanency Decisions

To truly empower LGBTQ youth, child welfare professionals must go beyond simply "prohibiting discrimination" against LGBTQ youth and seek to actively embrace and encourage them. Adults may feel that an LGBTQ youth may be too young to adequately assess issues related to their SOGIE, or that certain experiences are just a phase. When individuals, especially helping professionals and caretakers, second guess a youth's expressions related to SOGIE, this is often experienced as a form of rejection or shame. To empower LGBTQ youth, child welfare professionals should seek out a youth's expertise and insights when making major decisions about their permanency and well-being. Many LGBTQ youth in care have faced tremendous adversity in experiences with their families and in navigating a child welfare system that is often not as responsive and sensitive as one might hope. In their attempt at navigating those experiences, many LGBTQ youth develop a heightened sense of resilience and resourcefulness. As Gerald Mallon noted in his seminal work that first brought many of the issues facing LGBTQ youth in care to the forefront, this is a population with much more resilience than risk (Mallon, 1998). Child welfare professionals should develop a framework that seeks to utilize the strengths and resilience of LGBTQ youth when making crucial decisions about their future.

Ensure That LGBTQ Youth Are Not Isolated or Segregated from Other Youth

Placing a youth in their own room due to issues related to their SOGIE reinforces a dynamic in which LGBTQ youth feel isolated and marginalized. Child welfare professionals should work with foster parents and other caretakers to ensure that LGBTQ youth are included in decisions about bedroom and bathroom assignments. Child welfare professionals should not assume that just because a child identifies as gay, lesbian, or bisexual, they are unable to room with youth of the same sex. In addition, child welfare professionals should seek to ensure that transgender youth and gender nonconforming youth are placed appropriately on how they identify. Assigning a transgender or gender nonconforming youth to a bedroom or bathroom based solely on their assigned gender could be a very harmful and potentially unsafe experience.

Seek to Enhance the Peer Support System of LGBTQ Youth

Brené Brown (2006), who developed Shame Resilience Theory (SRT), defines shame as "the intensely painful feeling or experience of believing we are flawed and therefore unworthy of connection and belonging". A key component of cultivating shame resilience for LGBTQ youth is forming mutually empathetic and supportive relationships with others, which promotes connection and a sense of normalcy around the very same experiences that were previously their most isolating.

Service providers should be equipped to consider the impact of SOGIE in order to ensure peer support for LGBTQ youth. Double standards for LGBTQ youth can create barriers to peer support in numerous contexts.

Practitioners must be sensitive to the dynamics related to things such as dating rules, access to friends and peer groups, as well as access and support for extracurricular activities.

Ensure That Youth Are Acknowledged by the SOGIE They Identify With

In an effort to respect the dignity and worth of LGBTQ youth in care, child welfare professionals should ensure that all youth are acknowledged by the ways in which they identify and not by the ways in which others are most comfortable with identifying youth. Transgender and gender nonconforming youth deserve to be addressed by the gender they identify with and not by their assigned gender. Caretakers, professionals, teachers, and others should be reminded that transgender youth and gender nonconforming youth are in no way changing who they are or their identity, but rather the people around them are changing they ways in which they identify a youth. This approach helps others to recognize the need for sensitivity and competence to create an environment that is inclusive and affirming.

The sexual orientation of youth should be respected and acknowledged in similar ways. Staff, professionals, and others should ensure that LGBTQ youth are empowered to engage in normal developmental activities and experiences that any other youth would have access to. Gay and lesbian youth should be afforded the same privileges when it comes to romantic relationships, dating, and physical affection that straight youth are afforded. Under no circumstances should a youth be encouraged or pressured to engage in romantic relationships with members of the opposite sex.

Do Not Make Assumptions about a Youth's Sexual Orientation or Gender Identity

Child welfare professionals should be careful to not make assumptions about a youth's sexual orientation or gender identity. When first meeting with a youth, efforts to use language and terminology that is inclusive can help LGBTQ youth to feel a greater sense of comfort and safety. Simple modifications such as asking a youth if they are currently in a relationship or have a partner as opposed to asking if they have a boyfriend or girlfriend can be very effective in fostering sensitivity and acceptance. When meeting youth for the first time, child welfare professionals should be especially cautious not to assume that all youth are straight or cisgender. It is equally as important that child welfare professionals not make assumptions about a youth's sexual orientation or gender identity based solely on their external expressions of masculinity or femininity.

Recommendations for Child Welfare Agencies

LGBTQ youth come from families of all religious, political, ethnic, and economic backgrounds. Systems of care are made up of organizations of individuals, and these individuals often represent a variety of cultural, religious, and political experiences, values, and beliefs. No matter how LGBTQ-friendly a particular practitioner or organization is, social services have a history of participating in the stigmatization, discrimination, and ignorant treatment of the LGBTQ community. Creating a culturally competent organizational environment requires a commitment to comprehensive organizational change that addresses a measurable commitment and support from leadership, as well as a systems approach that considers service provision at all levels.

Routinely Train Staff on Issues Related to SOGIE

Even the most caring and sensitive child welfare professionals can benefit from enhancing their knowledge and skills when it comes to be affirming and competent to issues related to a youth's SOGIE. Agencies serving LGBTQ youth should seek to provide a strong foundational training on issues related to concepts, terminology, and experiences of LGBTQ youth. A recent survey of child welfare professionals found that most child welfare professionals have little or no formal training on LGBTQ identity and practice application (Wilson, Cooper, Kastanis, & Nezhad, 2014). Foundational trainings can help to enhance the competency and sensitivity of child welfare professionals, as well as to dispel any myths that they might have related to a youth's SOGIE.

Trainings that seek to increase the competency of child welfare professionals can help to strengthen confidence and comfort that is often necessary to engage in crucial conversations about a youth's SOGIE. The lack of comfort and confidence that many child welfare professionals experience contributes to a culture of silence that can be devastating for LGBTQ youth in care. By bringing issues related to youth SOGIE to the forefront, agencies can create a culture of inclusion and acceptance. Given the fact that many child welfare professionals have not openly discussed issues related to youth SOGIE, they are often unaware of their own actions that might be perceived by youth to be insensitive or even rejecting.

Trainings that allow child welfare professionals and other staff to explore their own biases or prejudices can prove to be very helpful in fostering a culture of inclusion. In many circumstances, child welfare professionals may not be aware of the ways in which socialization, society, and other factors might impact their ability to be sensitive and affirming. Topics that agencies might consider addressing in an attempt to create a more inclusive and affirming environment include:

- Basic terminology, concepts, and vocabulary related to SOGIE;
- Using inclusive language and respecting pronouns;
- Barriers to permanency that LGBTQ youth often encounter;
- Strategies for assessing and enhancing foster family acceptance;
- Barriers to acknowledging and addressing issues related to SOGIE;
- Self-reflection and self-assessment to identify personal biases and prejudice;
- Skills and strategies for preparing youth to come out;
- Skills and strategies to assist youth in dealing with rejection and stigma;
- Pathways into care that are common to LGBTQ youth;
- Distinguishing between traumatic stress responses and reactions to stigma, rejection, and discrimination;
- Establishing safety for LGBTQ youth in care; and
- Identifying community resources for LGBTQ youth.

*Modify Forms and Documents to Include Information
Related to SOGIE*

Some agencies or programs may consider preparing a confidential questionnaire that is provided to all youth at intake aimed at addressing areas related to SOGIE. Items to consider in confidential questionnaires might include:

- How youth view themselves in relation to SOGIE;
- Feelings and thoughts that youth might have about their SOGIE; and
- Ways in which staff, caretakers, and professionals can be empowering and sensitive to a youth's SOGIE.

Make LGBTQ Youth Aware of Their Rights

All youth in the child welfare system, regardless of their SOGIE, have the right to be protected from physical, sexual, and emotional harm. The purpose of the child welfare system is to protect youth from harm and future risk. For LGBTQ youth in care, their right to protection includes the right to be placed in a placement that is free of physical, sexual, and emotional maltreatment. Child welfare professionals must seek to make youth aware of their rights in placement, as well as the measures they can take when their rights have been violated or threatened.

Manage Confidential Information in Sensitive and Appropriate Ways

While maintaining and ensuring confidentiality is important when working with any youth, it can be especially important when working with LGBTQ youth. When child welfare professionals are made aware or sensitive information related to a youth's SOGIE, they must be sure to keep that information private and confidential. Child welfare professionals should not share sensitive information about a youth's SOGIE with colleagues, parents, or others without the youth's consent.

Adopt Antidiscrimination Policies

California was the first state to pass legislation that explicitly includes protections for LGBTQ youth in the foster care system. The California Foster Care Non-Discrimination Act went into effect in 2004, prohibiting discrimination in the California foster care system on the basis of several factors including sexual orientation and gender identity (California Welfare and Institutions Code, 2004). This policy mandated that group home administrators, public child welfare professionals, and foster parents complete training on topics related to sexual orientation, gender identity, and the rights of LGBTQ youth in care. Despite the fact that LGBTQ youth have received some attention at the state level, recent federal child welfare policy gains such as the Fostering Connections to Success Act have largely excluded LGBTQ youth (H.R. 4980, 2014). To date, no federal policies exist explicitly aimed at protecting LGBTQ youth in the child welfare system.

One recommendation that appears to be implemented with more and more frequency is the adoption of antidiscrimination policies. Child welfare agencies are encouraged to adopt written policies with wording that strongly forbids the discrimination, marginalization, and harassment of youth based upon sexual orientation or gender identity. Furthermore, these policies should be clearly conveyed to caregivers, staff, and any other professionals who will come into direct contact with youth in care. Items that agencies might consider when preparing antidiscrimination policies include:

- Verbal harassment such slurs, derogatory comments, jokes, or stereotypes;
- Physical harassment such as hitting, pushing, or slapping;

- Sexual harassment such as unwanted sexual advances;
- Responsibilities for reporting instances of harassment or discrimination;
- Privacy requirements when reporting instances of harassment or discrimination;
- Consequences of engaging in harassment or discrimination; and
- Whistle-blower policies that protect individuals who report harassment or discrimination.

Conclusion

The challenges and barriers that are often encountered by LGBTQ youth in the child welfare system have numerous layers of complexity. LGBTQ youth who come into contact with the child welfare system are entering a system that has only recently made any efforts toward being responsive to their needs. Little is known about the experiences of LGBTQ youth who navigate the child welfare system, and the information that is available suggests that much needs to be done to foster safety, acceptance, and normalcy for LGBTQ youth.

There is no question that despite the many disparities and challenges that LGBTQ youth in the child welfare system encounter, they are a population with much more resilience and resourcefulness than risk. It is critical that any efforts at the practice and policy levels aimed at creating a more inclusive and competent system seek to incorporate the resilience and resourcefulness of LGBTQ youth and former foster youth.

Societal acceptance for the rights of LGBTQ youth are at an all-time high, and many youth-serving institutions have made enormous strides in responding to the needs of LGBTQ youth and young adults. The time has come for the child welfare system to make similar strides by taking measures that aim to create a culture of inclusion and acceptance for LGBTQ youth. The stories of LGBTQ youth in care and alumni clearly point to the need for a heightened sense of awareness and acknowledgement of their presence. Similarly, efforts to recruit affirming foster and adoptive families as well as efforts to work with birth families on issues related to acceptance and the consequences of rejection would likely go a long way in establishing a greater sense of permanency and normalcy for LGBTQ youth. These efforts would largely address the overreliance on congregate care and other restrictive placement settings that has historically existed for LGBTQ youth.

Any efforts aimed to improve the conditions and experiences of LGBTQ youth must utilize a strengths-based framework that focuses more on their resilience than on their risks and deficits. Most LGBTQ youth who navigate the child welfare system have overcome overwhelming obstacles and challenges. It is not at all uncommon for LGBTQ youth in care to experience things like abuse, neglect, stigmatization, rejection, and discrimination. It is important that child welfare professionals and caretakers utilize an empowerment-based approach that utilizes the many strengths and resources that LGBTQ have developed in their experiences navigating a system that is often unwelcoming and unsafe.

ARTICLE REVIEWS

While the research on the experiences of LGBTQ youth in the child welfare system has been scarce, there have been a few studies in recent years that have been instrumental in creating a greater understanding of the issues facing LGBTQ youth in foster care. Increased attention aimed at better understanding the unique experiences of LGBTQ youth in the child welfare system will help to improve visibility of this population, as well as provide insights for future practice and policy efforts aimed at creating a more inclusive system of care.

The following section provides a synthesis of three recent studies that specifically address LGBTQ youth in foster care. Each study addresses different periods in the experiences of LGBTQ youth as they navigate the foster care system. One study provides incredible insights into the factors contributing to the disproportionate overrepresentation of LGBTQ youth in the child welfare system. Another study takes an in-depth look at the experiences that LGBTQ youth encounter while in foster care with a specific attention to foster family acceptance. A third study explores the many challenges and disparities that LGBTQ youth often face after aging out of the foster care system. For each study, a short summary is provided that specifically addresses the implications for LGBTQ youth in care.

SEXUAL AND GENDER MINORITY DISPROPORTIONALITY AND DISPARITIES IN CHILD WELFARE

A Population-Based Study[1]

Bianca D.M. Wilson and Angeliki A. Kastanis

While it has been assumed that LGBTQ youth are disproportionately overrepresented in the child welfare population, there have been no population-based studies to assess the exact rate of overrepresentation that exists. Prior to the publication of this study, evidence of LGBTQ youth disproportionality in the child welfare system was limited to practitioner accounts and non-administrative data such as alumni studies. This study is the first of its kind to specifically address the rates of overrepresentation of LGBTQ youth in the child welfare system. The study sought to answer two empirical questions:

1   What percent of foster youth are LGBTQ, and does value indicate disproportionality?
2   Are LGBTQ youth experiencing disparities in risks to permanency and well-being?

In order to accurately assess whether there is any empirical evidence of disproportionality, the researchers compared the rate of LGBTQ youth in the general population to the rate of LGBTQ youth in a foster care sample. Using a recent Daily Gallup survey, the researchers estimated that the rate of LGBTQ youth in the general population was 8.3%. When the researchers assessed a random sample of foster youth between the ages of 12 and 24, they identified that 19.1% of foster youth reported LGBTQ identities.

After identifying the percentage of foster youth who reported having LGBTQ identities, the researchers were able to create a Disproportionality Representation Index (DRI). The DRI for LGBTQ youth in the foster care system was estimated to be 2.3. This value indicates that LGBTQ youth are 2.3 times more likely to be placed in foster care than non-LGBTQ youth.

In addition to assessing the rate of disproportionality, this study also sought to examine whether LGBTQ youth experienced any disparities in factors associated with permanency and well-being. LGBTQ youth in the sample were much more likely to be placed in a group home than non-LGBTQ youth (25.7% vs. 10.1%). Furthermore, LGBTQ youth were much less likely to report that they were treated very well by the foster care system than their non-LGBTQ counterparts (51.10% vs. 61.02%). Homelessness rates were also assessed in this study. Just over 1 in 5 (21.09%) LGBTQ youth reported ever experiencing homelessness as compared to 13.90% of the non-LGBTQ sample.

Discussion

For decades, child welfare professionals and researchers have assumed that LGBTQ youth are disproportionately overrepresented in the foster care system. Because sexual orientation and gender identity have not been included in child welfare administrative data collection, the extent of overrepresentation has not been known. The rigorous design of this study provides child welfare professionals and researchers a much better idea about just how big a risk factor Sexual Orientation Gender Identity and Expression) are when it comes to the victimization experiences of LGBTQ youth. Findings suggest that LGBTQ youth are 2.3 times more likely to be placed in foster care than non-LGBTQ youth; therefore, child welfare policy professionals have strong evidence of the need to create policies and programs that are responsive to LGBTQ youth. With nearly one in every five teens in foster care reporting an LGBTQ identity, this is a population that can no longer overlooked or ignored.

In addition to providing strong evidence for programs and policies that are responsive to the needs and experiences of LGBTQ youth, the findings also provide evidence of the need for better tracking of child welfare data related to sexual orientation and gender identity. The Adoption and Foster Care Analysis and Reporting System has historically not included items aimed at assessing sexual orientation and gender identity, and the authors of this study suggest that data including SOGIE data would help to make LGBTQ youth much more visible.

Note

1 Reprinted with permission of Elsevier.

SEXUAL AND GENDER MINORITY DISPROPORTIONALITY AND DISPARITIES IN CHILD WELFARE

A Population-Based Study

Bianca D.M. Wilson and Angeliki A. Kastanis

Children and Youth Services Review 58 (2015) 11–17

1. Introduction

There are over 400,000 children in foster care and without permanent homes in the U.S. (Children's Bureau, 2015). Many child welfare advocates have noted that lesbian, gay, bisexual, transgender, and questioning (LGBTQ) youth are a significant subgroup of this population (Wilber, Ryan, & Marksamer, 2006). However, LGBTQ youth represent an unknown proportion of the total foster youth population, and it remains unclear whether there is evidence of disproportionality. Further, research on the experiences of LGBTQ youth in foster care indicate that they are exposed to unique risks associated with people's responses to their sexual orientation and/or gender identity (Mallon, 1998). Yet, we do not have population-based data on whether LGBTQ youth in foster care experience disparities. The need for more population-based data on LGBTQ youth in foster care was one of the primary conclusions of the recent Administration for Children and Families (ACF) Office of Planning, Research and Evaluation (OPRE) report on the human services needs among LGBT people (Burwick, Gates, Baumgartner, & Friend, 2014). In order for the child welfare system to fulfill its duty, it is critical that policymakers and caregivers have an understanding of the lives and unique challenges of the LGBTQ youth they serve.

Family rejection and violence are often cited as reasons for LGBTQ youth entering out-of-home care. Though no research study with foster youth has directly made this connection, research with youth experiencing homelessness indicates there may be some evidence for this theory. One study of homeless youth found that while both sexual minority and majority youth left their homes for similar reasons (family conflict, problems with family members, and desire for freedom), LGBQ youth left at nearly double the rate (Cochran, Stewart, Ginzler, & Cauce, 2002). Related studies have documented significant proportions of LGBTQ youth reporting verbal and physical violence within their families in response to their sexual and/or gender minority statuses (Hunter, 1990; Savin-Williams, 1994).

Rejection, abuse, and discrimination continue to affect LGBTQ youth while they are in out-of-home care. At various points in time while in the child welfare system these youth interact with case workers, foster parents, congregate care facility employees, and other foster youth. These encounters often include elements of anti-LGBT bias that can manifest as harassment and violence at the hands of other foster youth and caretakers, misconceptions of LGBTQ youth as sexual predators, attempts by foster parents to "cure" youth of their sexual or gender minority identity, and unfair isolation or discipline for otherwise age-appropriate conduct in group homes (Clements & Rosenwald, 2008; Mallon, 1998; Wilber et al., 2006). One study revealed that 56% of LGBT foster youth surveyed spent time on the streets because they felt safer there than in their group or foster home (Feinstein, Greenblatt, Hass, Kohn, & Rana, 2001). In addition to discrimination and safety concerns, practitioner accounts indicate that LGBTQ youth in foster care are less likely to find a permanent home (by reunification or adoption) than other youth, with transgender youth having the most difficult time achieving permanency (CASA, 2009; Mallon, 2009). These studies and advocate accounts are important perspectives for informing policies and practices; yet, a lack of population-level data on disparities limits the field's understanding of how pronounced these differences are within the child welfare system.

1.1. Claims of LGBTQ disproportionality in foster care

Across many practitioner accounts of the experiences of LGBTQ youth in foster care, there have been claims that this group is overrepresented in the child welfare system. Yet, no empirical studies published in peer-reviewed journals have been undertaken to directly assess evidence of LGBTQ disproportionality in foster care. Sexual orientation and gender identity are not standard parts of child welfare administrative data collection in the U.S. As such, non-administrative sources of data must be considered to answer questions about LGBTQ youth in foster care. There has been one self-published report ("The Midwest Study") on the economic, health and demographic characteristics (including sexual orientation) of young adults who were previously in foster care (Dworsky & Hall, 2013). The Midwest Study found that 11–15% of respondents identified as LGB, however the sampling methods do not allow for estimates of the population proportion. Another self-published report conducted by Tarnai and Krebill-Prather (2008) was particularly notable due to its larger sample size and aim to survey the entire population of a state child welfare agency. The study attempted to survey all of Washington State's foster care population to

assess basic demographics (including both sexual orientation and gender identity) and experiences in foster care
(Tarnai & Krebill-Prather, 2008). They found that 91% of
their sample identified as heterosexual, 2% identified as
gay or lesbian, 6% identified as bisexual, and 0.1% identified as transgender. Despite the strengths of this study,
the items used to measure sexual orientation and gender
identity are not those recommended by current scholars
on the topic (The GenIUSS Group, 2014; Sexual Minority
Assessment Research Team, 2009). Thus, there remains
a need for population-based research that appropriately
measures the proportion of foster youth who are LGBTQ
and examines their unique experiences in order to inform
allocation of child welfare resources and service provision.

1.2. Identifying the correct general youth LGBTQ population estimate

Assessing whether LGBTQ youth are overrepresented in
the child welfare system requires a comparison between
the proportion of LGBTQ youth in foster care and those
in the general population. For over three decades, extensive research on adolescent demographic characteristics
and behavior has been conducted via school-wide, state,
or national surveys. Starting in the mid-1980's, many of
these studies included questions about sexual orientation
(Reis & Saewyc, 1999; Remafedi, Resnick, Blum, & Harris, 1992; Russell & Joyner, 2001; Russell, Seif, & Truong,
2001). These studies likely included youth in foster care,
but did not specifically focus on that population, nor did
they report participants' dependency status. Literature
published in the U.S. report a range of estimates of the
percentage of the total youth population who are LGBTQ.
In an analysis of the largest sample of people asked directly about their sexual and gender minority status, Gates

and Newport (2012) reported that 6.4% of the U.S. adult population 18–29 years old identified as LGBT. The data used for these estimates were responses to the Gallup Daily tracking survey, which includes one item that asks whether the respondents identify as lesbian, gay, bisexual, or transgender — combining an assessment of sexual and gender minority status. Specific to youth, both the Youth Risk Behavior Surveillance System (YRBSS) and the National Longitudinal Study of Adolescent Health (Add Health Study) have provided estimates of sexual minority status among adolescents. Using YRBS data, Kann et al. (2011) assessed sexual orientation through both self-identification with a sexual minority label and sex of sexual partners across multiple states and districts that opted-in to include sexual orientation questions on their YRBS surveys. Though the exact wording of the sexual identity question varied among municipalities, they all used one question about which sexual identity label the respondents would choose for themselves, similar to the item used in this study. They estimated that, across the locations using a sexual orientation survey item, a median of 93% identified as heterosexual, 3.7% identified as bisexual, and 2.5% were unsure about their sexual identity, and 1.3% identified as gay or lesbian. Using Wave 1 of the Add Health data from 1995, Russell et al. (2001) found similar rates of sexual minority status through an assessment of responses to items about romantic attraction, similar to those used in the current study. Among adolescents who were 12–19 years old in 1995, they estimated that 7.4% of boys and 5.3% of girls reported some level of same-sex attraction. Taken together, these studies of sexual orientation using identity and attraction measures would suggest that sexual minority youth and young adults comprise between 6 and 8% of the U.S. youth population.

With regard to transgender status, population estimates are more challenging to identify because transgender status alone is not yet uniformly included on any national or statewide probability sample surveys of youth. However, some studies do provide estimates to consider in relation to the current study. For example, the Boston Youth Survey (BYS) conducted a probability survey of the city school district and used a single item approach to assess transgender status. Analyses of BYS reported in a peer-reviewed publication indicated that 17 out of 908 (1.7%) youth 13–19 years old identified as transgender (Almeida, Johnson, Corliss, Molnar, & Azrael, 2009). In a recent unpublished pilot using a nationally representative online survey, findings showed that 1.4% of the year 1 and 3.2% of the year 2 samples identified as transgender (Greytak, 2013). Taken together, these studies of transgender status within local probability surveys or national representative non-probability sample surveys would suggest that transgender youth make up somewhere between 1.3–3.2% of the U.S. youth population, but clearly more research is needed in this area.

1.3. Current study

The Los Angeles Foster Youth Study (LAFYS) was a one-time study conducted by the authors and their research team as part of their collaboration with the Recognize Intervene Support Empower (RISE) initiative, a five-year cooperative agreement awarded to the Los Angeles LGBT Center. This was one of six sites funded through the Permanency Innovations Initiative (PII; see, e.g., Permanency Innovations Initiative Training and Technical Assistance Project & Permanency Innovations Initiative Evaluation Team, 2013). RISE aimed to address barriers to permanency and wellbeing for lesbian, gay, bisexual, transgender and questioning (LGBTQ) youth in the child welfare system in Los Angeles County by decreasing anti-gay and anti-transgender bias in families and care-giving settings through the design of interventions. We designed the LAFYS to provide data that may inform the process of implementing and evaluating the interventions that RISE developed, and to answer core empirical questions about LGBTQ youth disproportionality and disparities. The current study presents findings for the primary empirical questions that guided the design of the study:

1 What percent of foster youth are LGBTQ and does this value indicate disproportionality?
2 Are LGBTQ youth experiencing disparities in risks to permanency and wellbeing?

In order to answer the first question on disproportionality, we also sought to use available population data to create a more precise estimate of LGBTQ youth in the general population.

2. Method

The LAFYS was conducted via computer-assisted telephone interviewing (CATI) between July–October 2013. Power calculations assuming that LGBTQ youth made up 15% of LGBTQ youth ages 12 + years with a 95% confidence interval and 2.5% margin of error indicated a needed sample of 765. Available resources prohibited attempting to contact the entire population, therefore, we drew a sample assuming an approximately 25% response rate to use as a contact list to recruit potential participants. The Los Angeles Department of Child and Family

Services (LA-DCFS) provided the contact information for a random sample of 2967 foster youth ages 12–21[1] years in out-of-home care in Los Angeles County. The LA-DCFS Research Department, Los Angeles County Family Court, and UCLA Institutional Review Board (IRB) reviewed and approved the project.

We used a stratified random sampling technique, where we split the sample into two age groups: 12–16 years and 17–21 years. We drew equal numbers of participants from these two groups in order to ensure a large enough sample within the older age group to make an accurate estimate of this LGBTQ subpopulation. Having an accurate estimate for this age range specifically allows us to make comparisons between past and future studies of youth transitioning out of foster care, many of which focus on youth ages 17 and older. In order to achieve this goal, we needed to oversample the older age group since they make up a smaller proportion of youth in foster care.

Westat, a national social science research firm, conducted the screening, obtained informed consent/assent, and administered the telephone interviews for LAFYS. Using the standard definitions published by the American Association for Public Opinion Research (AAPOR, 2011), the cooperation rate (CR4) was 65.7% and the response rate (RR4) was 41.8%. The refusal rate (RF3) was 21.9% and the contact rate (CT3) was 73.5%.

2.1. Participants

Youth were eligible to be included in the sampling frame if they: 1) were at least 12 years old, 2) were in "out-of-home" care,[2] 3) were not in juvenile detention, 4) had an address in the state of California, 5) were able to complete the survey in English, and 6) if the Child Welfare Services/Case

Management System had both an address and phone number for them. The LA-DCFS categorization of youth in "out-of-home" care, commonly referred to as foster youth, includes all youth who are dependents of the court living in residential or group care, foster homes, and kinship care (a type of placement where a child is placed in the home of a relative or a non-related extended family member). Although we provided informational material for youth and caregivers in both English and Spanish, the survey was only available in English. Table A1.1 provides details of the sample characteristics.

Table A1.1   **Unweighted demographics in LAFYS total sample**

	Total (n = 786)	
	Unweighted	
Age [mean in years (SD)]	15.88 (2.74)	
Race/ethnicity	n	%
Latino	434	56.1
American Indian	15	1.9
Asian/Pacific islander	22	2.8
Black	186	24.0
White	74	9.6
Bi/multiracial or ethnic	43	5.6
Born outside the U.S.	64	8.1
At least one bio parent born outside the U.S.	301	38.3
Placement type		
Group home	100	12.7
Relative/guardian	303	38.5
Foster home	373	47.4
Sex assigned at birth		
Male	332	42.2
Female	454	57.8

2.2. Procedures

Before the survey fielding began, we sent letters that included a \$2 pre-participation incentive to the randomly selected list of potential youth participants and their caregivers describing the project and providing potential participants an opportunity to contact us for questions. The letters also included a copy of "Survey FAQs" in English and Spanish, which answered some basic questions about the survey. Within a few days of sending the letters, Westat interviewers began calling youth. Assent was obtained from the youth directly. The actual CATI took approximately 20 min where the interviewer followed a computer-programmed script of the questionnaire. Every response used interactive voice response (IVR) technology that allowed for touch-tone responses to the questions over the phone for complete privacy.

2.3. Measures

The instrument was designed to assess demographic characteristics, experiences with various forms of discrimination, and rates of exposure to risks associated with challenges to permanency and wellbeing. Our final interview items drew from recently published reports focused on asking questions about sexual orientation and gender identity (The GenIUSS Group, 2014; Sexual Minority Assessment Research Team, 2009) and knowledge gathered from cognitive interviews and feedback groups with foster youth, LA-DCFS staff, caregivers, and providers.

2.3.1. SEXUAL ORIENTATION

Sexual orientation was measured using two of the three dimensions that define sexual orientation: identity and sexual attraction. We asked youth whether they considered themselves to be "straight or heterosexual, gay or lesbian, or bisexual". We also recorded a distinction between whether they were "not sure yet" what their sexual identity was (used to define "questioning" category) or they did not know what the question was asking. Attraction was measured using one item asking about romantic attraction to girls/women and another asking about romantic attraction to boys/men. Both items asked whether (options were: "yes", "no", or "I am not sure yet") they were romantically attracted to that gender.

2.3.2. GENDER IDENTITY

According to the Center of Excellence for Transgender Health (CETH), gender identity is best captured in a survey by using a two-part series of questions that asks about a person's sex assigned at birth and their current sex or gender (Sausa, Sevelius, Keatley, Iñiguez, & Reyes, 2009). The GenIUSS Group (2014) report also advocates for this item structure. This two-step method captures a person's sex/gender history while also validating their current gender identity. The first item asked "What sex were you assigned at birth (what the doctor put on your birth certificate)?" and the options were "male" or "female." The second item asked "When you think about how you see yourself now, which of the following terms best fits how you describe your gender?" and the options were ("boy", "girl", "transgender", or "I am not sure yet"). Slightly deviating from previously tested approaches, we added "I am not sure yet" to the gender identity question options in order to again distinguish between youth who may be questioning their identity and those who would be coded as "I don't know" because they are unfamiliar with the terms or concept of gender identity.

2.3.3. RISKS TO PERMANENCY AND WELLBEING

The questionnaire also included items about youth's experiences with the foster care system. This section was comprised of questions that asked about the youth's time in foster care, the number of placements in which they have lived, and the type of placements (group home, foster home, etc.). We included several items about experiences known to be connected with risks to not achieving permanency and risks to overall wellbeing. For example, as a measure of whether physical and psychological distress had been experienced, we asked whether they had ever been hospitalized and, if so, whether the reasons had been psychological, physical, or both. Additionally, we asked whether they had ever experienced homelessness, interactions with the criminal system or police, and negative schooling outcomes, such as suspension or expulsion. A majority of these items have been used in other surveys that focus on youth, particularly youth in the foster care or juvenile justice system (Irvine, 2010).

2.4. Weighting and analysis

Sampling designs used to ensure large enough sample sizes of subgroups (e.g., over sampling an age group) and patterns of non-responses among various subgroups may bias the data. To address this, we used sample weights. Weighting is a strategy for adjusting the data to compensate for design and response issues. Using a two-stage procedure, we weighted the sample to match the Los Angeles foster youth population aged 12–21 years. The first stage of weighting corrected for the different probabilities of selection associated with the number of youth in foster care in either the 12–16 year old or 17–21 year old age groups (i.e., design weight). The weighting of this first stage takes into account the higher probability of a youth being selected if they are in the older age group, than if they were in the younger age group. The second stage accounted for the differences in proportions between males and females within the sample compared to the population (i.e., post-sampling weight). This second stage takes into account the proportion of female and male respondents as compared to the female/male ratio in the foster care population. The final weight created was a product of the design weight (age group) and sampling weight (sex).

We used SPSS and Stata statistical software to complete descriptive and inferential analyses (IBM Corp., 2013; StataCorp., 2013). Sample sizes are reported for each variable and proportions are reported using the total number of non-missing responses as the denominator.

3. Findings

3.1. Disproportionality

In order to determine whether there is evidence of disproportionality, we had to first determine the appropriate estimate of LGBTQ status in the general youth population and then create an estimate of LGBTQ status within the foster youth sample. These values are then used to calculate a Disproportionality Representation Index (DRI). This value operates much like an odds ratio in that a 1.00 indicates equal values of the data points being compared. In this case, a population estimate within the foster care population was compared to a population estimate of the general population. Values above and below 1.00 indicate degrees of overrepresentation and underrepresentation, respectively. Previously, the DRI has primarily been applied to analyses of racial disproportionality within the foster care system (Morton, Ocasio, & Simmel, 2011). However, this index has not been calculated for LGBTQ youth in foster care.

3.1.1. GENERAL POPULATION

To estimate the number of LGBT youth and young adults in the general population, we used data from the Gallup Daily tracking survey. Data from the ongoing Gallup Daily tracking survey has recently been used to estimate the percentage of U.S. adults who identify as LGBT nationally, in addition to state by state LGBT estimates (Gates & Newport, 2012). These data are based on telephone interviews conducted from June 2012 to June 2014, with a random sample of 373,352 adults, aged 18 and older, living in all 50 U.S. states and the District of Columbia. The interviews were conducted with respondents on landline telephones and cellular phones, with interviews conducted in Spanish for respondents who are primarily Spanish-speaking. Though the age range for the Gallup Daily tracking survey does not include minors or those who are questioning or unsure of their identity, we are able to estimate the LGBT identity rate for respondents, age 18 to 24, who live in Los Angeles County. Thus, these data allow us to provide the most current and closest estimate of LGBT identity rates to compare to foster youth in Los Angeles County between the ages of 12 to 21.

Our analysis focused on the sample of 865 young adults (ages 18–24) in the Gallup Daily tracking survey. We used the survey design weights supplied by Gallup to estimate the proportion of young adults in Los Angeles County that answered "yes" to the question "Do you, personally, identify as lesbian, gay, bisexual or transgender?." According to our analysis, 8.3% of young adults in Los Angeles County between the ages of 18 and 24 identify as LGBT (95% conf. interval: 6.5%, 10.6%).

3.1.2. FOSTER YOUTH POPULATION

To create a single estimate of LGBTQ youth in foster care, we added together the youth in each of these sexual and gender minority groups, removing overlap created by respondents who fit more than one category (e.g., a transgender lesbian-identified youth would only be counted once in this overall estimate of LGBTQ youth). Using Fig. A1.1 to identify the subpopulations that make up the intersections of these three variables, conceptually, the LGBTQ status count = a + b + c + d + x + y + z.

We identified that 19.1% of the youth in this county's foster care population were LGBTQ. The weighted estimates of respondents who were LGBQ-identified, same-sex attracted, and transgender are shown in Table A1.2a. We also provide weighted demographics of youth included in the combined LGBTQ status in Table A1.2b.

3.1.3. DISPROPORTIONALITY REPRESENTATION INDEX (DRI)

Using the Gallup Daily tracking data, this study estimates that 8.3% of young adults in the general population are LGBT. Further, using data from the LAFYS, we estimate that 19.1% of foster youth ages 12–21 years identify as LGBTQ. As such, the DRI for LGBTQ youth in foster care in this county is 2.3. This value indicates that LGBTQ youth are highly overrepresented in out-of-home care.

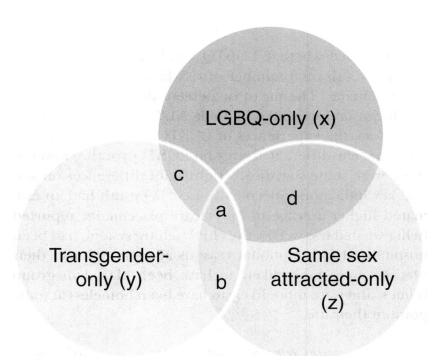

Figure A1.1 **Calculating LGBTQ status**

Table A1.2 **Population proportion estimates of sexual and gender minority statuses**

	Proportion estimate/ sample size	95% confidence interval	
		Lower limit, upper limit	
LGBTQ	19.1%/n = 684	16.26, 22.03	
LGBQ	13.4%/n = 758	11.04, 15.76	
Transgender	5.6%/n = 756	3.95, 7.24	
Same-sex attracted	13.2%/n = 739	10.83, 15.49	

3.2. Disparities

We examined whether LGBTQ youth differed from non-LGBTQ youth on a number of risk factors to permanency and wellbeing. The mean or percent differences for each risk factor are presented in Table A1.3. On most measured indicators, the experiences of LGBTQ youth in foster care do not seem different from non-LGBTQ youth. However, there were some statistically significant differences on several key indicators. Specifically, LGBTQ youth had an estimated higher average of foster care placements, reported being treated less well by the child welfare system, had been hospitalized for emotional reasons at some point in their lifetime, were more likely to have been placed in group homes, and were more likely to have been homeless at some point in their life.

Geometric means reported; conducted test of mean difference with log transform of outcome variable to adjust for highly skewed data.

4. Limitations

A key limitation of this study is that there is no available probability sample in which both sexual orientation and gender identity (as one item or separately, including questioning youth) are identified for this exact county and age group, which we can then compare to the LGBTQ foster youth data. Thus, it is possible that the DRI is affected by the comparison to only young adults in the county who do not report being unsure or questioning of their LGBT status in the general population. However, we anticipate that this bias creates an underestimate of the DRI as questioning youth were a small fraction of LGBTQ youth in the LAFYS and young adults

Table A1.3 Differences between LGBTQ and non-LGBTQ on risks to permanency and wellbeing

Factor	Mean (se) or %		Test statistic
	LGBTQ	Non-LGBTQ	
Total # of placements[a]	2.85 (1.1)	2.43 (1.03)	t(682) = 2.19*
# of placements in last year	1.05 (.14)	.89 (.07)	t(682) = 1.07
Total years in foster care	5.56 (.50)	5.20 (.22)	t(682) = .65
Currently in group home	25.7%	10.1%	F(1, 682) = 23.84*
Treatment by foster care system			F(3.00, 2044.44) = 3.57*
Very well	51.10%	61.02%	
Somewhat well	35.14%	32.87%	
Not very well	12.93%	5.78%	
Hospitalized	38.80%	31.17%	F(1, 682) = 2.97[†]
Reason for hospitalization			F(3.99, 2724.52) = 7.81*
Emotional reasons	13.47%	4.25%	
Physical reasons	13.60%	21.87%	
Emotional and physical reasons	11.04%	4.16%	
Ever been arrested	25.74%	22.17%	F(1.97, 1345.69) = 0.49
Ever been homeless	21.09%	13.90%	F(2.00, 1362.72) = 4.57*
Times suspended from school	.73 (.57)	.57 (.11)	t(682) = .76
Times expelled from school	.16 (.16)	.05 (.02)	t(682) = .70

Note. Standard deviations appear in parentheses next to the means.

in the foster youth sample were more likely to identify as LGBTQ than those under 17. If that pattern holds for the general population, then the estimate we use from the Gallup Daily tracking survey is higher than one that would be achieved by including those under 17, therefore driving the DRI to be lower than if we had a fully matched comparison group.

Another challenge is that the survey was only available in English. This was appropriate given the limits of resources which made conducting field tests of multiple versions of the survey in various languages unfeasible. However, we recognize that this may have reduced our understanding of LGBTQ foster youth who do not comprehend English at a level that made them eligible for the survey, particularly in LA County.

Finally, it is important to recognize that these estimates were derived from a study of one large urban county child welfare service department. It is possible that levels of disclosure of sexual and gender minority statuses are higher and levels of experienced anti-gay/bisexual and anti-transgender bias are lower in urban areas where there are ongoing efforts to improve the service and social climates for LGBTQ youth. In particular, the specific location in which these data were collected have existing state and county-level non-discrimination policies that protect children and caregivers with regard to sexual orientation, gender identity or expression (Non-Discrimination Policy in Placement Decisions, 1200–500.00, 2014; Cal. Assemb. B. 458, 2003–2004). However, more research is needed to understand the experiences of foster youth in other locations and to assess the usefulness of the methodology and generalizability of the results beyond Los Angeles County.

5. Discussion

This article provides initial evidence that lesbian, gay, bi-sexual, transgender, and questioning youth in the foster care population are both overrepresented and experiencing unique risks to permanency and wellbeing. The majority of youth within the LGBTQ foster youth population were youth of color and over half were girls, indicating that many of them likely face multiple forms of discrimination and disparities. Future research needs to examine how subgroups of LGBTQ youth may experience foster care differently. For example, transgirls may be especially vulnerable to discrimination based on gender conformity as studies show that parents have a stronger negative reaction to gender atypicality among male-assigned at birth children (D'Augelli, Grossman, & Starks, 2008; Galambos, Almeida, & Petersen, 1990) and transgirls are often more visible in organizational systems (Irvine, 2010). Similar to research on racial disparities within child welfare (Morton et al., 2011), future research is needed to better understand at what points in care disproportionality and disparities occur, and how this may differ by subgroup of LGBTQ youth.

LGBTQ youth were more likely to have been hospitalized in general, and significantly more likely to have been hospitalized for emotional reasons. Although the time of hospitalizations were not assessed, prior studies have shown that identity-specific stressors contribute to higher rates of depression, mood disorders, and suicidality among LGBTQ youth, which may be related to being hospitalized for emotional reasons (Meyer, Frost, & Nezhad, 2014; Spirito & Esposito-Smythers, 2006). Unmet mental health needs may also be an additional barrier to permanency for LGBTQ youth if caregivers are less likely to be accepting of youth in emotional distress. Additionally, LGBTQ respondents were more likely to have been homeless at one point. This is consistent with previous evidence that LGBTQ youth leave their homes at nearly double the rate of non-LGBTQ youth (Cochran et al., 2002) and may choose to spend time on the streets because they felt safer there than in their group or foster home (Feinstein et al., 2001). Finally, within the institutional context, LGBTQ youth reported being treated less well by the child welfare system, moving around to more placements, and were more likely to have been placed in a group home or residential facility. The significance of these findings is supported by previous scholarship that has linked multiple placements, mental health concerns, homelessness, and placements in group homes as barriers to permanency faced by all youth, and LGBTQ youth in particular (Jacobs & Freundlich, 2006). Though the study was not designed to provide direction to practitioners or policymakers on how best to resolve these disparities, the findings provide evidence of several areas on which future applied research could focus.

The study also demonstrates that questions about sexual orientation and gender identity can be asked among foster youth specifically, as they have for decades in large-scale general population research. However, by identifying a feasible survey methodology for documenting population-level disproportionality, the study also highlights a major gap in the field of child welfare research – the absence of administrative data on sexual orientation and gender identity. A lack of systematic data collection has likely contributed to the invisibility of LGBTQ youth in the system, thus making policies aimed at strengthening administrative data collection systems to include these variables important next steps. We recognize that the Children's Bureau Division of Policy is currently considering changes to the Adoption and Foster Care Analysis and Reporting System (AFCARS) (AFCARS Proposed Rules, 2015) and this may be one of the areas in which changes are made if variables documenting sexual orientation and gender identity are included. Just like for any other minority or underserved group, collecting demographic data that make LGBTQ youth populations visible helps policymakers and providers understand disparities and make informed resource allocation decisions. However, given the vulnerability of LGBTQ youth within systems of care, precautions must be taken to collect only data that are needed and to protect confidentiality of the information (Wilber, 2013).

Acknowledgments

We greatly appreciate the project Co-Investigator, Khushnuma Cooper, for comments on early versions of the paper. The design and data collection phases of this study were funded by the Children's Bureau, Administration on Children, Youth and Families, Administration for Children and Families, U.S. Department of Health and Human Services, under grant number 90-CT-0154, via the Los Angeles LGBT Center. The contents of this report are solely the responsibility of the authors and do not necessarily represent the official views of the Children's Bureau or the Los Angeles LGBT Center.

References

AFCARS Proposed Rules; HHS AFC 2015, 80 Fed. Reg. No. 26 (proposed February 9, 2015).

Almeida, J., Johnson, R.M., Corliss, H.L., Molnar, B.E., Azrael, D. (2009). Emotional distress among LGBT youth: The influence of perceived discrimination based on sexual orientation. *Journal of Youth and Adolescence*, 38 (7) (2009), pp. 1001–1014

American Association for Public Opinion Research (2011). *Standard definitions: Final dispositions of case codes and outcome rates for surveys* (7th edition), AAPOR, Deerfield, IL: AAPOR

Burwick, A., Gates, G., Baumgartner, Friend, S.D. (2014). Human services for low income and at-risk LGBT populations: An assessment of the knowledge base and research needs OPRE Report Number 2014–79, Office of Planning, Research and Evaluation, Administration for Children and Families, U.S. Department of Health and Human Services, Washington, DC.

Cal. Assemb. B. 458 (2003–2004), Chapter 331 (Cal. Stat. 2003).

CASA (2009). Helping courts serve the best interests of LGBTQ youth. Casa connections newsletter. National Court Appointed Special Advocate Association, Seattle, WA.

Children's Bureau (2015). The AFCARS Report: Preliminary Estimates for FY 2011 as of July 2012. Retrieved on June, 2015 at http://www.acf.hhs.gov/sites/default/files/cb/afcarsreport19.pdf

Clements, J.A., Rosenwald, M. (2008). Foster parents' perspectives on LGB youth in the child welfare system, *Journal of Gay & Lesbian Social Services*, 19 (1) pp. 57–69

Cochran, B.N., Stewart, A.J., Ginzler, J.A. (2002). Challenges faced by homeless sexual minorities: Comparison of gay, lesbian, bisexual, and transgender homeless adolescents with their heterosexual counterparts, American Journal of Public Health, 92 (5) pp. 773–777

D'Augelli, A.R., Grossman, A.H. & Starks, M.T. (2008). Gender atypicality and sexual orientation development among lesbian, gay, and bisexual youth, Journal of Gay & Lesbian Mental Health, 12 (1–2), pp. 121–143

Dworsky, A., Hall, C. (2013). The Economic Well-being of Lesbian, Gay, and Bisexual Youth Transitioning Out of Foster Care (No. 7635), Mathematica Policy Research, Princeton, NJ

Feinstein, R., Greenblatt, A. Hass, L., Kohn, S., & Rana, J. (2001). Justice for all? a report on lesbian, gay, bisexual and transgendered youth in the New York juvenile justice system, Lesbian and Gay Project of the Urban Justice Center, New York

Galambos, N.L., & Almeida, D.M., Petersen, A.C. Masculinity, femininity, and sex role attitudes in early adolescence: Exploring gender intensification, Child Development, 61 (6) pp. 1905–1914

Gates, G. F. Newport, F. *Special report: 3.4% of US adults identify as LGBT.* Gallup, Inc. (2012)

The GenIUSS Group. (2014). Best practices for asking questions to identify transgender and other gender minority respondents on population-based surveys. J.L. Herman (Ed.). Los Angeles, CA: The Williams Institute.

Greytak, E. (2013). How do you ask the question? Assessing sex and gender in a national sample of adolescents. Paper presented at the 27th Annual American Evaluation Association, Washington D.C.

Hunter, J. (1990). Violence against lesbian and gay male youths, Journal of Interpersonal Violence, 5 (3) pp. 295–300

IBM Corp. Released 2013. IBM SPSS statistics for windows, version 22.0. Armonk, NY: IBM Corp.

Irvine, A. (2010). "We've had three of them": Addressing the invisibility of lesbian, gay, bisexual and gender nonconforming youths in the juvenile justice system. Columbia Journal of Gender and Law, 19 (1) (2010), pp. 675–702

Jacobs, M. Freundlich, M. (2006). Achieving permanency for LGBTQ youth, 85, Child Welfare (2006), pp. 299–316

Kann, L. O'Malley Olsen, E., T. McManus, T., Kinchen, S. Chyen, D. Harris, W., Wechsler, H. (2009). Sexual identity, sex of sexual contacts, and health-risk behaviors among students in grades 9–12: Youth risk behavior surveillance, selected sites, United States, 2001–2009. Morbidity and Mortality Weekly Report (MMWR), 60 (SS07) pp. 1–133

Mallon, G.P. (Ed.), (2009). Social work practice with transgender and gender variant youth, Routledge, New York, NY

Meyer, I.H., Frost, D.M., Nezhad, S. (2014). Minority stress and suicide in lesbians, gay men, and bisexuals. In P.B. Goldblum, D. Espelage, J. Chu, B. Bongar (Eds.), The challenge of youth suicide and bullying, Oxford University Press, New York, NY (2014), pp. 177–190

Morton, C.M., Ocasio, K., Simmel, C. (2011). A critique of methods used to describe the overrepresentation of African Americans in the child welfare system Children and Youth Services Review, 33 (9), pp. 1538–1542 ArticlePDF (230KB)

Non-Discrimination Policy in Placement Decisions, 1200–500.00 DCFS child welfare policy manual. Los Angeles County Department of Children and Family Services (2014)

Permanency Innovations Initiative Training and Technical Assistance Project & Permancy Innovations Initiative Evaluation Team. The PII approach: Building implementation and evaluation capacity in child welfare. U.S. Department of Health and Human Services, Administration for Children and Families, Children's Bureau & Office of Planning, Research and Evaluation, Washington, DC (2013).

Reis, B., Saewyc, E.M. (1999). Eighty-three thousand youth: Selected findings of eight population-based studies as they pertain to anti-gay harassment and the safety and wellbeing of sexual minority students. Safe Schools Coalition of Washington

Remafedi, G., Resnick, M., Blum, R., Harris, L. (1992). Demography of sexual orientation in adolescents. *Pediatrics*, 89 (4), pp. 714–721

Russell, S.T., Joyner, K. (2001). Adolescent sexual orientation and suicide risk: Evidence from a national study, *American Journal of Public Health*, 91 (8), pp. 1276–1281

Russell, S.T., Seif, H., Truong, N.L., (2001). School outcomes of sexual minority youth in the United States: Evidence from a national study. *Journal of Adolescence*, 24 (1), pp. 111–127 ArticlePDF (153KB)

Russell, S.T., Joyner, K. (2001). Adolescent sexual orientation and suicide risk: Evidence from a national study, American Journal of Public Health, 91 (8) pp. 1276–1281

Sausa, L.A., Sevelius, J., Keatley, J., Iñiguez, J.R. Reyes, M. (2009). Policy recommendations for inclusive data collection of trans people in HIV prevention, care & services

San Francisco, CA: Center of Excellence for Transgender HIV Prevention: University of California, San Francisco

Savin-William, R.C. (1994). Verbal and physical abuse as stressors in the lives of lesbian, gay male, and bisexual youths: Associations with school problems, running away, substance abuse, prostitution, and suicide, Journal of Consulting and Clinical Psychology, 62 (2), p. 261

Sexual Minority Assessment Research Team (2009). Best practices for asking questions about sexual orientation on surveys. The Williams Institute, Los Angeles, CA.

Spirito, A., Esposito-Smythers, C. (2006). Attempted and completed suicide in adolescence, Annual Review of Clinical Psychology, 2, pp. 237–266

StataCorp. (2013). Stata statistical software: Release 13, StataCorp LP, College Station, TX (2013)

Wilber, S. (2013). Guidelines for managing information related to the sexual orientation and gender identity and expression of children in child welfare systems, putting pride into practice project. Family Builders by Adoption, Oakland, CA

Wilber, S., Ryan, C., Marksamer, J. (2006). CWLA best practice guidelines, Child Welfare League of America, Washington, DC: Child Welfare League of America.

FUNCTIONAL OUTCOMES AMONG SEXUAL MINORITY YOUTH EMANCIPATING FROM THE CHILD WELFARE SYSTEM[1]

Svetlana Spiegel and Cassandra Simmel

The challenges and obstacles facing foster care alumni have been closely examined in a number of rigorous studies in recent years. While these studies have highlighted the adversities that foster care alumni often face, little attention has been given to the specific experiences of sexual minority youth emancipating from foster care. This study was the first to look specifically at the role that sexual orientation and gender identity play in experiences of youth emancipating from foster care.

Using data from the Multi-Site Evaluation of Foster Youth Programs, the researchers compared the victimization experiences, child welfare experiences, as well as the functional outcomes (education, employment, economic well-being, and homelessness) of youth preparing to emancipate from foster care.

Similar to findings in several other studies, sexual minority youth in this study were much more likely to report living in congregate care or group home settings (32.1% vs. 19.1%). In addition, sexual minority youth in this study reported experiencing more placement disruptions than heterosexual youth (6.44% vs. 3.98%).

The functional outcomes of sexual minority youth emancipating from foster care in the current study varied significantly from those of heterosexual youth in this study in a number of domains. Sexual minority youth were much less likely to obtain a high school diploma than their heterosexual counterparts (43% vs. 63%). Similarly, sexual minority youth reported lower rates of employment (73%) when compared to heterosexual youth (88%).

Two findings from this study provide strong evidence of the need for child welfare professionals to better prepare LGBTQ youth for independence. Sexual minority youth were less likely to report having a checking account (19% vs. 44%), and only 19% of sexual minority youth reported having a vehicle as compared to 33% of heterosexual youth.

Perhaps one of the most significant findings for child welfare professionals and caretakers was in the area of housing stability. Sexual minority youth were more than twice as likely (2.41) to experience homelessness than heterosexual youth. When the researchers found that the likelihood that a sexual minority youth would experience homelessness increased significantly with each placement disruption and victimization experience.

This study is the first of its kind to provide evidence of the disparities that many LGBTQ youth face as they transition into adulthood. Many foster alumni encounter adversity after aging out, and LGBTQ youth are especially vulnerable to many of those adversities. LGBTQ youth emancipating care are especially vulnerable to housing instability and homelessness. Although this study did not assess the size and scope of the social support systems of youth emancipating from care, the increased vulnerabilities provide further evidence of the need to create stronger and more intimate support systems for LGBTQ youth.

Note

1 Reprinted with permission of Elsevier.

FUNCTIONAL OUTCOMES AMONG SEXUAL MINORITY YOUTH EMANCIPATING FROM THE CHILD WELFARE SYSTEM

Svetlana Shpiegel and Cassandra Simmel

Children and Youth Services Review, 61 (2016) pp. 101–108

1. Introduction

Since the early 1990s, researchers, child welfare professionals and legislators have worked to systematically address the difficulties foster care alumni experience relative to their non-foster care peers. There is substantial research documenting the challenges and obstacles faced by foster care alumni, ranging from interpersonal, psychosocial, and health challenges to difficulties in fulfilling age-pertinent achievements, such as completing higher education, securing consistent employment and living in stable and independent environments (Barth, 1990; Courtney, 2009; Courtney & Dworsky, 2006; Iglehart & Becerra, 2002; Montgomery, Donkoh, & Underhill, 2006; Simmel, Shpiegel, & Murshid, 2012; Wolanin, 2005). Much of this work has been instrumental in addressing the process by which foster youth transition out of the child welfare system, as well as in identifying gaps that persist following the passage of the Foster Care Independence Act of 1999 (commonly referred to as the Chafee Act). The Chafee Act is notable for broadening the scope and type of transitional services and supports provided to foster youth, as well as the age of eligibility for receipt of these services (National Foster Care Awareness Project, 2000). In essence, these program modifications recognized that preparation for adulthood requires an initiation of sustained support delivered to youth early in adolescence and not simply a flurry of training exercises just as youth are about to depart the system.

These policy advances notwithstanding, the heterogeneity of youth involved with the child welfare system makes it difficult to establish the extent to which functional outcomes (i.e., housing; education; employment) are equivalent across all members of this population, or whether specific sub-groups of foster care alumni are more disadvantaged than others. This is an important and timely concern as many states have modified and expanded their child welfare services to better address the broad needs of adolescents, including service provision during the typically vulnerable phase of transition to adulthood (Children's Bureau's, 2013). For instance, many states have expanded the age at which youth can remain involved with the child welfare system, or opt to re-open system involvement (Children's Bureau's, 2013). These changes hint at the arguably protective nature of many child welfare programs geared toward this age group. However, it is necessary to examine variations in outcomes among different subgroups to understand how existing services and programs can be refined to promote positive functioning for all foster care alumni. For this paper, we use data from the Congressionally mandated project entitled Multi Site Evaluation of Foster Youth Programs to explore the challenges that a specific sub-group – sexual minority youth – face, in comparison to their heterosexual peers. We focus on measurements of key independent living outcomes to get a broad picture of how sexual minority youth fare during the transition from foster care to independence.

1.1. Brief overview of relevant policy and federal initiatives

This project is partially informed by two federal policy actions for foster youth: the Chafee Act and the more recent Information Memorandum (IM) of 2011 (Administration for Children and Families {ACF}, 2011). The Chafee Act replaced the former federal Independent Living structure that was in place to serve foster youth as they prepared to depart the child welfare system. Following the passage of the Chafee Act, states could elect to provide services, namely the provision of Medicaid and housing assistance, to youth after the age of 18 (generally until age 21). And, critically, funding for expanding the services and programs for transitioning youth was increased (National Foster Care Awareness Project, 2000). Thus the Chafee Act reflects a remarkable shift in states' focus and responsibility for foster youth transitioning to adulthood, including a commitment to promoting self-sufficiency.

Furthermore, in 2011, the Children's Bureau issued an Information Memorandum that outlined the need for ensuring best practices within the child welfare system such that states are actively and effectively "protecting and supporting" sexual minority youth while they are in foster care. The IM is explicit in conveying that states need to improve best practices in addressing sexual minority youths' safety and permanency needs. We argue that a logical extension of the 2011 IM and the 1999 Chafee Act mandates is to ensure that sexual minority youth are receiving effective preparation for life after leaving foster care. However, little information currently exists about the outcomes of sexual minority youth as compared to their heterosexual peers. Understanding the extent of challenges faced by these youth is critical for a successful implementation of both pieces of federal action.

1.2. Gaps in services for sexual minority youth

There is a strong basis for focusing on the outcomes solely for sexual minority youth who are involved with the child welfare system. While the transition to adulthood encompasses a set of risks for most foster care alumni, sexual minority youth may face additional challenges and perils. Recent research as well as policy memos and legal briefs and reviews reveal the extent to which sexual minority youth contend with stressors presumably connected to their sexual orientation: rejection by biological families (Elze, 2014; Khoury, 2007; Tamar-Mattis, 2005; Yarbrough, 2012); lack of permanency (Mallon, Aledort, & Ferrera, 2002; Wilbur, Ryan, & Marksamer, 2006; Yarbrough, 2012); victimization by peers (Freundlich & Avery, 2004; Gallegos et al., 2011); placement in restrictive settings (Child Welfare Information Gateway, 2013; Khoury, 2007; Sullivan, Sommers, & Moff, 2001; Tamar-Mattis, 2005); and, insufficient or absent support from staff, foster parents, and caseworkers (ACF, 2011; Elze, 2014; Gallegos et al., 2011; Mallon et al., 2002; Nolan, 2006; Sullivan et al., 2001; Tamar-Mattis, 2005).

First, sexual minority youths' involvement with child welfare services may directly stem from family conflicts surrounding sexual orientation, resulting in irrevocable dislocation from family members. Entry into the child welfare system may be instigated by biological families' rejection of youths' sexuality (Elze, 2014; Khoury, 2007; Mallon et al., 2002), which may also constrain opportunities for reunification once in out-of-home care. As Elze (2014)notes, "(U)nlike their heterosexual and gender-conforming peers, LGBTQ youths often face familial rejection in response to their sexual orientation and/or gender identity and gender expression. Heterosexism in families can directly result in the youth's ejection from the home, or it can exacerbate other parental problems, heightening familial conflict until the youth is kicked out or leaves" (p. 162).

Second, compounding their obstacles in reunifying with biological families, sexual minority youth are at enhanced risk for placement disruptions, which can be attributable to numerous factors, namely peer victimization within youths' living environments (Elze, 2014; Freundlich & Avery, 2004; Mallon et al., 2002; Sullivan et al., 2001), stigmatization for their sexual orientation (ACF, 2011; Freundlich & Avery, 2004; Khoury, 2007; Tamar-Mattis, 2005), and lack of appropriate foster parents who can provide safe, stable, and supportive homes (Mallon, 2011). Numerous studies and law reviews have documented the chronic verbal and physical mistreatment many sexual minority youth endure from their peers while in out-of-home care (Estrada & Marksamer, 2006; Tamar-Mattis, 2005). Though sexual minority youth are the victims in these situations, they are nonetheless the ones to repeatedly move, in search of a safe out-of-home living arrangement. This may result in placement in more restrictive settings such as congregate care, despite the fact that such a placement is implemented for purposes of personal safety and not for therapeutic reasons (Child Welfare Information Gateway, 2013; Elze, 2014).

Further complications ensue for youth as a result of inappropriate placement in institutionalized living arrangements. For instance, placements in restrictive settings are generally for "difficult cases," which inappropriately sweeps sexual minority youth under this label. In turn, such a label could have negative implications for reunification possibilities with families as well as for placements in more family-like settings. Moreover, residing in restrictive settings could result in running away from out-of-home placement and child welfare protection altogether (Elze, 2014; Freundlich & Avery, 2004; Nolan, 2006). Homelessness, of course, exposes youth to an additional set of risk elements, further hampering early adulthood outcomes (Nolan, 2006).

A third factor associated with sexual minority status is the absence of adults who can provide emotional support and acceptance. One consequence of impermanent living situations and/or placement in congregate living is the obstruction of opportunities for youth to develop nurturing and stable relationships with caregivers, staff, potential mentors, and others who are instrumental for both formal and informal delivery of preparation for adulthood (Freundlich & Avery, 2004; Mallon, 2011; Nolan, 2006). In addition, staff and caseworkers' interactions with sexual minority youth may range from inadequate to harmful. Some caseworkers and staff may have a cursory understanding of youths' sexual orientation and their personal needs while other staff may actively ostracize them and prevent them from engaging in necessary services (Nolan, 2006; Sullivan et al., 2001). Finally, the lack of mentors for all child welfare-involved youth is a recognized challenge (Renne & Mallon, 2014); for sexual minority youth, it potentially heightens their troubled trajectories for aging out of the system.

1.3. How do sexual minority youth fare in the transition to adulthood?

Although sexual minority youth share many commonalities with their heterosexual counterparts in that they all are contending with traumatic backgrounds, disrupted childhoods, and impaired interpersonal relationships with adults and caregivers (Child Welfare Information Gateway, 2013), they also represent a somewhat distinct group. This group has a great deal to manage while involved with child welfare system—unsafe and inconsistent living environments, chronically severed ties with family members, peer victimization, and rejection by those who are assigned to care for them and provide support. These factors may contribute to deficiencies in the quality of care afforded them, resulting in insufficient support for a great number of issues, including attention to the transition into young adulthood. In addition, their time in foster care may hasten the onset of or exacerbate mental health difficulties, further compounding post-transition outcomes. Ultimately, if sexual minority youth face a unique array of challenges while in the child welfare system, what happens to these youth after they depart the system? At present, very few studies have examined this question, resulting in a paucity of information on this topic (research by Dworsky, 2013 is one notable exception). In this descriptive investigation, we focused on the following two central aims as guides for our inquiry of the MEFYP dataset.

1   Do sexual minority youth (who are in the process of aging out or are recent foster care alumni) differ from heterosexual youth (also imminent or recent foster care alumni) on educational attainment, employment, economic wellbeing and homelessness?

2   Does sexual orientation relate to the above-mentioned outcomes controlling for youths' demographics, victimization histories, and child welfare experiences?

2. Methods

2.1. Dataset and procedure

This research is based on a secondary analysis of data from the Congressionally mandated Multi-Site Evaluation of Foster Youth Programs (MEFYP), a randomized-controlled study designed to assess the effectiveness of four independent living programs in California and Massachusetts. The current investigation utilizes data from the Life Skills Training program (LST) of Los Angeles County.[2] This program provides life skills instruction and case management to foster youth ages 16 and older. As part of the evaluation project, youth were interviewed at baseline (age 17) and once each year after that (i.e. ages 18 and 19) for a total of three waves of data collection (U.S. Department of Health and Human Services, 2008).

Youth were considered eligible for MEFYP if they were 17 years old, placed in out-of-home care, and deemed appropriate for LST. A total of 482 youth were eligible for inclusion; at baseline, 97% of the eligible youth were interviewed. Of those interviewed at baseline, 91% were interviewed at the first follow-up and 88% were interviewed at the second follow-up. Detailed information about the design and procedures of the MEFYP evaluation can be found in previously published work (see Greenson, Garcia, Kim, Thompson, & Courtney, 2015; U.S. Department of Health and Human Services, 2008).

2.2. Sample

For our study, all youth who participated in the three waves of data collection (i.e. ages 17, 18, and 19) and had valid information on sexual orientation at baseline were included in the analysis (N = 405, 84% of the original sample). No differences on gender, race or ethnicity were found between participants and the excluded youth. The final sample consisted of 161 males and 244 females (40.0% and 60.0% respectively). The majority of youth were African American (N = 180, 44.4%), followed by Whites (N = 135, 33.3%), American–Indians/Alaska Natives (N = 39, 9.6%), multiracial (N = 29, 7.2%), Native Hawaiian/Other Pacific Islander (N = 8, 2.0%) and Asian (N = 1, .2%) In addition, 175 youth (43.2%), irrespective of race, identified as Hispanic or Latino.

2.3. Measures

In our study, four sets of variables were included in the analysis: (1) demographics and sexual orientation; (2) victimization histories; (3) child welfare experiences; and (4) functional outcomes (i.e. education, employment, economic well-being, and homelessness). Information about demographics, victimization histories, and child welfare factors was obtained from the baseline interview (age 17); information about outcomes was obtained from the second follow-up interview (age 19). Missing data were present for several variables, resulting in a modest decrease in sample size for some analyses.

2.3.1. DEMOGRAPHICS

Gender was coded as either male or female. Ethnic identity was defined as Hispanic or non-Hispanic, and race was defined as either white or non-white (all minority race categories, including "multiracial", were designated as "non-white").

2.3.2. SEXUAL ORIENTATION

Youth were asked to self-identify as heterosexual, homosexual, bisexual, or "something else". Those who identified as homosexual, bisexual or "something else" were designated as "sexual minority" for the purpose of our study.

2.3.3. VICTIMIZATION

This variable represented a sum of 16 dichotomous (yes/no) items asking about the ways in which caregivers may have mistreated the youth before their first entry into foster care. Examples included "Did your caregivers often fail to provide regular meals for you so that you had to go hungry or ask other people for food"; "Did any of your caregivers ever throw or push you, for example, push you down a staircase or push you into a wall"; and "Did any of your caregivers ever lock you in a room or closet for several hours or longer".

2.3.4. SEXUAL ABUSE

Youth were asked if anyone ever touched or kissed them against their will, or attempted to do so; and if anyone ever had intercourse, oral sex or anal sex with them against their will, or attempted to do so. Youth who responded "yes" to any of these questions were designated as having a history of sexual abuse.

2.3.5. CHILD WELFARE EXPERIENCES

Youth were asked about their current placement types, as well as placement changes, school transitions, and independent living preparation/services received.

2.3.6. CURRENT PLACEMENT TYPE

Placement type at baseline was coded as: (1) with relatives; (2) non-relative foster home; (3) group home/

residential treatment facility; and (4) other setting (e.g. with a friend or roommate, friend's family, homeless shelter).

2.3.7. PLACEMENT CHANGES

This variable represented the total number of foster homes, group homes or residential treatment facilities youth lived in since first entering foster care.

2.3.8. SCHOOL TRANSITIONS

This variable represented the number of times youths changed schools because their family moved, or because they changed foster care placements.

2.3.9. INDEPENDENT LIVING PREPARATION/SERVICES

This variable was a sum of 21 dichotomous independent living services youth may have received throughout their lifetimes (formally or informally). The services covered five broad domains: (1) leadership development (e.g. involvement in leadership activities, mentoring other youth); (2) educational services (e.g. ACT/SAT preparation, assistance with college applications); (3) employment services (e.g. help with resume writing, assistance with job interviewing skills); (4) financial literacy services (e.g. help on the use of a budget, help balancing a checkbook); and (5) daily living skills (e.g. training on personal hygiene, meal planning and preparation).

2.3.10. FUNCTIONAL OUTCOMES

Four broad outcome domains served as dependent variables in the analyses. As previously noted, information on all outcomes was obtained from the second follow-up interview (i.e. when youth were about 19 years old).

2.3.11. EDUCATIONAL ATTAINMENT

Youth were asked if they obtained a high school diploma or GED. This variable was dichotomously coded as either "yes" or "no".

2.3.12. EMPLOYMENT

Youth were asked about their current employment, as well as about past employment experience. A dichotomous variable representing *any* employment between the ages of 17 and 19 (yes/no) was used as an outcome indicator.

2.3.13. ECONOMIC WELLBEING

To assess economic wellbeing, youth were asked about their financial assets, financial hardships and receipt of financial assistance. Financial assets included having a checking account, a savings account and a vehicle (each coded yes/no). Financial hardships included experiencing *any* of the following difficulties in the past year (yes/no): begging for money; making money by recycling cans, bottles or other items; selling blood or plasma; selling personal possessions; and going hungry. In addition, youth were asked how they perceived their own financial situation – response options were "saving a little money each month", "just getting by", or "struggling to make it". Finally, youth were asked about receipt of public financial assistance during the past year, including TANF, WIC benefits, food stamps, SSI, general relief payments or other welfare payments (each coded yes/no). Importantly, most questions pertaining to economic wellbeing were asked only of those youths who were legally emancipated at the time of the second interview (i.e. age 19).

In addition to the above-mentioned indicators, a dichotomous variable representing a relatively stable financial situation was constructed. Youth who had a checking account, who avoided financial hardships and defined their situation as either "saving each month" or "getting by," and who did not receive public financial assistance, were considered financially stable. In contrast, those who did not have a checking account, who experienced at least one financial hardship, "struggled to make it" financially, or received public assistance, were considered financially unstable. This variable was used as an outcome indicator in multivariate analyses.

2.3.14. HOMELESSNESS

Youth were asked if they were currently homeless or resided at a homeless shelter. In addition, they were asked if during the past 12 months they stayed overnight at a hotel, motel or Single Room Occupancy; in a car, truck or some other type of vehicle; or in an abandoned building, on the street, or outside somewhere. Youth who responded "yes" to any of these questions were considered to possess a history of homelessness.

2.4. Analytic strategy

Data analysis was conducted in several steps. First, univariate analyses were performed to describe youths' demographics, victimization histories and child welfare experiences, as well as their functional outcomes at age 19 (i.e. education, employment, economic wellbeing and homelessness). Next, bivariate analyses (i.e. chi-square tests and t-tests) were conducted to examine the relationships between youths' sexual orientation and the study variables. At the final step, a series of binary logistic regressions were performed to assess the contribution of sexual orientation to educational attainment, employment, financial stability and homelessness. In each regression equation, independent variables were entered in four blocks: (1) gender, race and ethnicity; (2) victimization and sexual abuse; (3) placement instability, school transitions and independent living services; and (4) sexual orientation. This order of entry reflected an interest in examining the contribution of sexual orientation over and above possible variations in youths' demographics and prior experiences. All analyses were performed in SPSS version 21.0.

3. Results

3.1. Sample description

About 60% of youths in the present sample were female; 64% were non-white, and 43% were Hispanic. In addition, 20% identified as sexual minority (i.e. homosexual, bisexual or "something else"). Participants had an average of 2.35 victimization experiences prior to entering foster care, and about 34% reported a history of sexual abuse. At baseline (i.e. age 17), over 40% lived with relatives, one-third resided in non-relative foster homes and one-fifth were placed in group homes or residential treatment facilities. Furthermore, participants reported 4.31 different placements (i.e. foster homes, group homes and/or residential treatment facilities) during their stay in foster care, as well as 4.27 school transitions. Finally, an average of 9 independent living services were received by the youth throughout their lifetimes (see Table A2.1).

By age 19, nearly 60% of youths obtained a high school diploma or GED. Additionally, over 80% obtained some work experience between the ages of 17 and 19. Nevertheless,

Table A2.1 **Descriptive Statistics of the Study Sample (N = 405)**

Variable	Heterosexuals	Sex minorities	Overall
	% or mean (SD)	% or mean (SD)	% or mean (SD)
Demographics			
Female	59.0	65.4	60.2
Non-white	65.4	66.2	63.5
Hispanic	42.0	50.6	43.2
Victimization histories			
Victimization	2.24 (3.17)	2.78 (3.42)	2.35 (3.22)
Sexual abuse	31.7	43.2	33.6
Child welfare experiences			
Baseline placement type			
With relatives	42.9	40.7	42.5
Non-relative foster	34.3	25.9	32.6
Group home/res.	19.1	32.1	21.7
Other setting	3.7	1.2	3.2
# of placements	3.98 (4.40)	5.62 (6.44)	4.31 (4.91)
# of school transitions	4.08 (5.19)	5.05 (4.66)	4.27 (5.10)
# of IL services	9.39 (5.01)	9.06 (4.91)	9.33 (4.99)

Note: Missing data for each variable ranged from 0% to 5%.

about 1 in 4 received public financial assistance, 1 in 6 had a history of homelessness and 1 in 3 experienced some financial hardship (i.e. one or more) during the past year. In addition, only half of youths had a checking account, slightly over one-third had a savings account and just over 30% had a vehicle. Overall, merely one-fourth of youths were considered financially stable based on the composite variable described in the Methods section (see Table A2.2).

Table A2.2   **Bivariate Differences in Youth Functional Outcomes at age 19 (N = 405)**

Variable	Heterosexuals %	Sex minorities %	Overall %	χ2
High school diploma/GED	63.0	43.2	59.0	9.65**
Employment	88.2	73.4	85.3	9.89**
Homelessness	11.7	25.9	14.6	9.38**
Public financial assistance	25.7	45.0	29.4	7.76**
Checking account	54.3	30.4	49.6	13.62***
Savings account	43.7	19.0	38.8	15.24***
Vehicle	33.3	18.8	30.4	5.77*
Financial hardship (≥ 1)	32.1	48.3	35.3	4.87*
"Struggles to make it"	14.9	30.0	17.9	6.49*
Financially stable (composite)	27.6	12.2	24.3	6.70*

Note: Missing data for each variable ranged from 0% to 5% (with the exception of some financial indicators, where missing data was about 25% due to their relevance to emancipated youth only).

3.2. *Bivariate differences between heterosexuals and sexual minority youth*

Sexual minority youth were not significantly different from heterosexual peers on gender, race and ethnicity, as well as on victimization histories. Nevertheless, a salient trend revealed that they had slightly higher rates of sexual abuse

(43.2% versus 31.7%; χ^2 = 3.34, p = .06), as well as somewhat different placement types at baseline (χ^2 = 7.69, p = .053). Specifically, sexual minority youth were less likely than heterosexuals to reside in non-relative foster homes (25.9% versus 34.3%), and more likely to live in group homes or residential treatment facilities (32.1% versus 19.1%). Furthermore, they tended to report increased number of placements (M = 5.62 versus M = 3.98; t = – 2.69, p < .05), though no significant differences were found in the number of school transitions or independent living services received (see Table A2.1).

When outcomes at age 19 were examined, sexual minority youth were less likely than heterosexual youth to obtain a high school diploma or GED (43% versus 63%; χ^2 = 9.65, p < .01) and to have employment experience between the ages of 17 and 19 (73% versus 88% respectively; χ^2 = 9.89, p < .01). Furthermore, they were more likely to receive public financial assistance (45% versus 26%; χ^2 = 7.76, p < .01), and less likely to have a checking account (30% versus 54%; χ^2 = 13.62, p < .001), savings account (19% versus 44%; χ^2 = 15.24, p < .001) and a vehicle (19% versus 33%; χ^2 = 5.77, p < .05). Sexual minority youth were also more likely to experience homelessness (26% versus 12%; χ^2 = 9.38, p < 01) and less likely to be financially stable (12% versus 28%, χ^2 = 6.70, p < .05) (see Table A2.2).

3.3. Logistic regression analyses: relationship between sexual orientation and outcomes

Table A2.3 summarizes the results of four logistic regressions examining the relationships between youths' sexual orientation and outcomes at age 19 (i.e. education, employment, financial stability and homelessness). Demographic variables, victimization histories and child welfare experiences were controlled in the analyses. All models were statistically significant and deemed appropriate for the data based on Hosmer and Lemeshov test.

Table A2.3 **Logistic Regression Analyses: Associated Characteristics with Outcomes at age 19**

	Diploma/ GED	Employment	Homelessness	Financial stability
	(N = 355)	(N = 353)	(N = 355)	(N = 300)
	OR	OR	OR	OR
Variable	*(CI)*	*(CI)*	*(CI)*	*(CI)*
Gender	1.67*	.85	.73	.93
	(1.02–2.73)	(.43–1.67)	(.36–1.48)	(.51–1.67)
Race	.91	1.14	.85	.66
	(.51–1.59)	(.55–2.37)	(.39–1.85)	(.35–1.26)
Ethnicity	.81	.71	.99	1.75
	(.47–1.38)	(.35–1.44)	(.47–2.08)	(.94–3.26)
# Victimization	1.05	1.03	1.13**	1.01
	(.97–1.14)	(.93–1.14)	(1.03–1.24)	(.92–1.11)
Sexual abuse	1.10	1.03	.88	1.46
	(.64–1.88)	(.51–2.09)	(.41–1.88)	(.79–2.70)
# Placements	.94^	.98	1.12***	.94
	(.89–1.00)	(.91–1.06)	(1.05–1.20)	(.87–1.02)
# School transitions	.96	1.06	.95	1.00
	(.91–1.01)	(.96–1.17)	(.88–1.04)	(.93–1.07)
# IL services	1.09***	1.10**	.95	1.05^
	(1.04–1.14)	(1.03–1.18)	(.89–1.02)	(.99–1.11)
Sexual orientation	.46**	.45*	2.41***	.41*
	(.26–.80)	(.23–.88)	(1.20–4.85)	(.18–.90)

3.3.1. EDUCATIONAL ATTAINMENT

Sexual minority youth were less than half as likely as hetero-sexual youth to obtain a high school diploma or GED (OR =.46, p <.01), even after controlling for demographics, victimization histories and child welfare experiences. Furthermore, females (OR = 1.67, p <.05) and those who received more independent living services (OR = 1.09, p <.001) were more likely to obtain a high school diploma/GED. Specifically, being a female increased the likelihood of obtaining a high school diploma or GED by 67%, while each additional independent living service received resulted in about 10% increase. Finally, a strong trend has indicated that placement instability was associated with somewhat lower rates of high school/GED completion (OR =.94, p =.055).

3.3.2. EMPLOYMENT

Although the final model (i.e. with four blocks of independent variables) was statistically significant and deemed appropriate for the data, only sexual orientation and receipt of independent living services were associated with having work experience. Identifying as a sexual minority decreased one's likelihood of having work experience by more than 50% (OR =.45, p < .05), whereas each additional independent living service received increased such likelihood by 10% (OR = 1.10, p < .01). Noteworthy, the contribution of sexual orientation was significant even after controlling for demographics, victimization histories and child welfare experiences (including the receipt of independent living services).

3.3.3. HOMELESSNESS

Identifying as a sexual minority emerged as a strong predictor of homelessness (OR = 2.41, p < .05), even after controlling for demographic indicators, victimization histories and child welfare experiences. Sexual minority youth were more than twice as likely to experience homelessness as their heterosexual peers. Additionally, increased victimization in youths' original families (OR = 1.13, p < .01) and higher placement instability (OR = 1.12, p < .001) were associated with experiencing homelessness. Specifically, each additional victimization experience, as well as each additional placement change, increased the likelihood of homelessness by more than 10%.

3.3.4. FINANCIAL STABILITY

Sexual orientation was the only statistically significant predictor of financial stability (i.e. having a checking account, avoiding financial hardship and receipt of public assistance, and either "saving each month" or "just getting by") in the final model. Identifying as a sexual minority decreased youths' likelihood of being financially stable by over 50% (OR = .41, p < .05) even after other independent variables were controlled. Receipt of more independent living services was associated with higher likelihood of financial stability, though this result failed to reach significance level (OR = 1.05, p < .058).

4. Discussion

The goal of this project was to measure sexual minority youths' functional outcomes at age 19, relative to those of their heterosexual peers. The rationale for a detailed focus on sexual minority youth stems from the likelihood that their young adulthood lives may be compromised as a result of factors related to representing a "largely invisible population within child welfare systems" (Elze, 2014, p. 160). Moreover, though the state of research on sexual minority youth during their involvement with child welfare is deemed "growing yet still insufficient" (Gallegos et al., 2011, p. 232), research on their lives immediately following emancipation is virtually non-existent. Our intention with this study was to address some of this informational vacuum. From a policy perspective, our study is informed by both the Chafee Act and the Children's Bureau 2011 Information Memorandum, with their respective emphasis on the expansion of independent living services and the need for best practices in attending to the needs of sexual minority youth involved with the child welfare system.

Using data from one site of the Multi-Site Evaluation of Foster Youth Programs (MEFYP) study, our bivariate findings indicate that the deficits for sexual minority youth are noteworthy across all categories of functional outcomes. That is, in comparison to same-age heterosexual peers, this group demonstrates significantly lesser functioning in education, employment, housing stability, and financial matters. Specifically, regarding the financial status of the two groups, sexual minority youth were more likely to experience financial hardships and indicate that they were "struggling to make it." Correspondingly, sexual minority youth were less likely to be "financially stable", and possess checking or savings accounts, and more likely to use public assistance. For related functional well-being indicators, sexual minority youth were less likely to have high school diplomas/GEDs and work experience, and more likely to experience homelessness compared to their heterosexual counterparts.

That the sexual minority youth in our study would experience financial difficulties and homelessness may be at least partially related to their relatively low rates of high school completion. Yet, interestingly, the one indicator in which this group fares the best across all of the outcomes is employment experience. Though the percentage of sexual minority youth with work experience was lower than the percentage of heterosexual youth with work experience, just under three-quarters of the former had at least some experience between the ages of 17 and 19. Nevertheless, we did not measure the length and stability of employment for either group, or the income level derived from it. Perhaps sexual minority youth are characterized by more unstable work patterns, or lower paying employment, as a result of their lower rates of high school completion. This factor and other related financial indicators could at least partially explain the differential outcomes we observed.

Although quantitative studies on the outcomes of sexual minority youth who are recent foster care alumni are mostly absent from the research literature, we located one recent study that provides some context for our findings. In Dworsky's (2013) research using data from the Midwest Evaluation of the Adult Functioning of Former Foster Youth, she explored economic well-being outcomes of LGB youth and heterosexual peers at age 21 years, with 11% of the 591 youth self-identified as LGB. In the results, statistically significant differences were observed on some economic indicators such as use of public assistance and economic hardships. Yet, there were critical divergences from our findings too. For instance, the Midwest study did not uncover any statistical differences between the two groups on items related to education, employment status (excluding financial earnings), and homelessness. While this lack of congruence between our study and the Midwest study on a comparable set of outcomes is perplexing, there are notable distinctions between the studies that can partially explain these discontinuities. Specifically, the larger sample of sexual minority youth in our study, coupled with possible geographic differences in child welfare program-ming, services for sexual minority youth and general avail-ability of resources, could be influential in this regard. Furthermore, participants in our sample were, on average, two years younger than those reported on in the Midwest study. It is possible that disparities in outcomes in terms of education, employment and housing stability diminish as youth mature.

After ascertaining that between-group differences existed in our study, we set out to examine factors that may be asso-ciated with why the sexual minority group was faring worse than their heterosexual counterparts. We conducted multi-variate analyses to examine how multiple factors, including placement and abuse history, number of school and living transitions, and sexual orientation affected youths' subse-quent functioning. As previously noted, sexual minority youth who are under the auspices of the child welfare system frequently receive unequal, hostile, or inappropriate treat-ment relative to their heterosexual peers (ACF, 2011; Elze, 2014; Gallegos et al., 2011; Mallon et al., 2002; Nolan, 2006; Sullivan et al., 2001; Tamar-Mattis, 2005). This context un-derscores how the risks sexual minority youth face potentially influence a cascade of interrelated negative events, giving rise to deficits in services for this group. Of note, the lack of permanency and inconsistent placement settings for this pop-ulation could lead to a host of parallel challenges ultimately resulting in inadequate preparation for self-sufficiency as young adults (Elze, 2014; Freundlich & Avery, 2004; Mallon, 2011; Sullivan et al., 2001). The results from our analytic model, however, indicate that sexual orientation was associ-ated with each category of functional outcomes even when controlling for other important factors. Therefore, sexual orientation was an independent factor that increased the odds of youths' poorer outcomes. According to our data, it is not the youths' lack of permanency in and of itself, but perhaps the challenges associated with these placements that could be at play. For instance, relational difficulties – namely, bullying by peers – may inhibit effective participation in preparatory programs for independent living, as well as in educational settings.

Although some of the systemic and peer relational factors may have played a role in the observed discrepancies in outcomes, it is important to consider other elements that may influence negative outcomes. These include challenges related to histories of abuse, current mental health functioning, and the broader societal treatment of sexual minority youth, who may endure homophobia beyond the child welfare system. It should also be noted that the present sample is predominantly African–American and Hispanic. Only 8.3% of youths were non-Hispanic Whites, much lower than the percentage reported in other studies of foster youth, including the Midwest study (Dworsky, 2013). It is possible that the combined circumstances of being racial/ethnic minority, as well as sexual minority, negatively affected youths' functioning. This explanation is aligned with existing research pointing to substantial challenges often faced by racial and ethnic minority youth who identify as LGBTQ (Craig, McInroy, Austin, Smith, & Engle, 2012). This points to an area in which future research is greatly needed. Specifically, larger samples are needed to examine possible interactive effects between youths' race/ethnicity and sexual orientation in relation to functional outcomes.

4.1. Limitations and future directions

The findings of this study should be interpreted in light of several limitations. First, the sample was restricted to a single county in one state, and may not have been representative of all youth in foster care. Second, we examined youth' sexual orientation at baseline only (i.e. when they were age 17) and did not account for possible changes in self-identification in subsequent waves. Third, findings are limited by the attrition of some youth between the baseline (i.e. age 17) and age 19 interview. Furthermore, some questions (e.g. financial outcomes) were asked only of youth who have legally emancipated by age 19, further limiting the sample size available for analysis. Fourth, because there are no commonly accepted guidelines for measuring financial stability among emancipating foster youth, we relied on somewhat subjective definition of this construct in the present study. Finally, factors not included in our analyses may have contributed to variations in outcomes between heterosexuals and sexual minority youth. For instance, we did not examine youths' mental health or involvement in risky behaviors (e.g. substance use) which could have contributed to variations in functional outcomes. We also did not measure variations in the amount of contact with and support from biological family members. Existing research indicates that foster youth tend to reconnect with biological family during the period of transition to adulthood, and often rely on these family members for support and guidance (Courtney, 2009). Sexual minority youth, however, might not have the same opportunities to reconnect with biological family members due their rejection of youths' sexuality. Overall, we are cautious about the findings we report here as we emphasize that we cannot directly ascertain why sexual minority youth manifest more negative outcomes as young adults.

In turn, these limitations lead to avenues for additional research in this topic area. As noted, future studies should examine how factors such as mental and physical health, as well as interpersonal issues related to sexual orientation (lack of concrete support or mentoring), lead to compromised outcomes upon exiting the system. Moreover, the field needs a longitudinal examination – over a substantially greater duration of time – of the independent living outcomes for sexual minority youth so that measurements of functioning could occur across a broader developmental period. It is conceivable that the immediate transitional period is complicated for this group, but this may stabilize over time. If so, examining the factors that contribute to such stabilization is particularly important. Additionally, it is important to examine how youths' sexual orientation may change over time, and how these changes may affect subsequent functioning. Relatedly, the current dataset did not specifically identify transgender youth, thus, research on this vulnerable subgroup is sorely needed. Overall, perspectives directly from sexual minority youths, particularly on how they perceive their own needs and challenges, as well as how their capacity for resilience and positive growth can be furthered, would add immeasurably to this topic. Finally, research on appropriate definitions and measurement strategies for financial stability outcomes among emancipating foster youth could also be beneficial.

5. Conclusion

Overall, this research adds to the literature on the unique risks that sexual minority youth face as imminent or recent graduates of the child welfare system. Findings may contribute toward developing effective interventions for this vulnerable sub-group of youth, as emphasized by recent federal actions (ACF, 2011). Across all functional indices measured, sexual minority youth had significantly lower outcomes relative to their heterosexual peers. However, more research is needed to examine the factors that influence these unequal outcomes. It is important for future research to identify how and why specific factors interfere with sexual minority youths' preparation for and eventual functioning as young, independent adults.

Acknowledgments

We are grateful to Holly Larabee and Elliott Smith from the National Data Archive on Child Abuse and Neglect at Cornell University for their technical assistance and support. We are further thankful to Mike Pergamit, Mary Bruce Webb, and Maria Woolverton for guidance on the background of the Multi-site Evaluation of Foster Youth Programs. Finally, we appreciate the time and effort that the youth participants contributed toward the MEFYP project so that future generations of foster youth could learn from their experiences.

The data used in this publication were made available by the National Data Archive on Child Abuse and Neglect, Cornell University, Ithaca, NY, and have been used with permission. Data from *Multi-Site Evaluation of Foster Youth Programs (Chafee Independent Living Evaluation Project), 2001–2010* were originally collected by: Mark E. Courtney; Matthew W. Stagner; and Michael Pergamit. Funding for the project was provided by Office of Planning, Research and Evaluation and the Children's Bureau Administration for Children and Families, U.S. Department of Health and Human Services Washington, D.C. (Award Number(s): 233-02-0059). The collector(s) of the original data, the funder(s), NDACAN, Cornell University and their agents or employees bear no responsibility for the analyses or interpretations presented here.

References

Barth, R.P. (1990). On their own. Child and Adolescent Social Work, pp. 419–440.

Child Welfare Information Gateway (2013). Supporting your LGBTQ youth: A guide for foster parents. Washington, DC:US Department of Health and Human Services, Children's Bureau.

Children's Bureau (2013). Fostering connections factsheet, volume 14(2), Child Welfare Information Gateway.

Commissioner, Administration for Children and Families (2004). Lesbian, gay, bisexual, transgender and questioning youth in foster care. Information memorandum (**ACYF-CB-IM-11-03**), United States Department of Health and Human Services, Washington, D. C.

Courtney, M.E. (2009). The difficult transition to adulthood for foster youth in the U.S.: Implications for the state as corporate parent. Social Policy Report, 23 (1).

Courtney, M.E., Dworsky, A. (2006). Early outcomes for young adults transitioning from out-of-home care in the USA. Child and Family Social Work, 11, pp. 209–219.

Craig, S.L., McInroy, L., Austin, A., Smith, M., Engle, B. (2012). Promoting self-efficacy and self-esteem for multiethnic sexual minority youth: An evidence-informed intervention. Journal of Social Service Research, 38 (5), pp. 179–189.

Dworsky, A. (2013). The economic well-being of lesbian, gay, and bisexual youth transitioning out of foster care OPRE Report #2012–41, Office of Planning, Research, and Evaluation, Administration for Children and Families, U.S. Department of Health and Human Services, Washington, DC.

Mallon, G.P., McCartt Hess, P. (2014). (Eds.), Child welfare for the 21st century: A handbook of practices, policies, and programs (2nd ed.), Columbia University Press, New York City, NY, pp. 158–178.

Estrada, R., Marksamer, J. (2006). Lesbian, gay, bisexual, and transgender young people in state custody: Making the child welfare and juvenile justice systems safe for all youth through litigation, advocacy, and education, Temple Law Review, 79, pp. 415–438.

Freundlich, M., Avery, R. J. (2004). Gay and lesbian youth in foster care: Meeting their placement and service needs, Journal of Gay & Lesbian Social Services, 17 (4), pp. 39–57.

Gallegos, A., White, C.R., Ryan, O'Brien, K., Pecora, P.J., Thomas, P. (2011). Exploring the experiences of lesbian, gay, bisexual, and questioning adolescents in foster care, Journal of Family Social Work, 14, pp. 226–236.

Greenson, J.K.P., Garcia, A., Kim, M., Thompson, A.E., Courtney, M.E. (2015). Development and maintenance of social
support among aged-out foster youth who received independent living services: Results from the Multi Site Evaluation
of Foster Programs, Children and Youth Services Review, 53,
pp. 1–9.

Iglehart, A., Becerra, R. (2002). Hispanic and African American youth:
Life after foster care emancipation. Social Work with Multicultural Youth, 11, pp. 79–107.

Mallon, G.P., Aledort, N., Ferrera, M. (2002). There's no place like
home: Achieving safety, permanency, and well-being for lesbian
and gay adolescents in out-of-home care settings, Child Welfare,
51, pp. 407–439.

Montgomery, P. Donkoh, C., Underhill, K. (2006). Independent living programs for young people leaving the care system. The
state of the evidence. Children and Youth Services Review, 28,
pp. 1435–1448.

Nolan, T.C. (2006). Outcomes for a transitional living program
serving LGBTQ youth in New York City. Child Welfare, 85 (2),
pp. 385–406.

Renne, J., Mallon, G.P. Unpacking permanency for youth: Overuse/mis-
use of another planned permanent living arrangement (APPLA)
as a permanency goal. In Mallon, G.P., McCartt, P., and Hess, P.
(Eds.), Child welfare for the 21st century: A handbook of practices, policies, and programs (2nd ed.), Columbia University Press,
New York City, NY (2014), pp. 455–466

Simmel, C., Shpiegel, S., Murshid, S.N. (2012). Foster care alumni and
postsecondary support: Exploring variation in state support. Journal of Policy Practice, 12, pp. 43–61.

Sullivan, C., Sommers, S., Moff, J. (2001). Youth in the margins: A report on the unmet needs of lesbian gay, bisexual, and transgender
adolescents in foster care. Lambda Legal Defense and Education
Fund, New York.

Tamar-Mattis, A. Implications of AB458 for California LGBTQ youth
in foster care. Law & Sexuality Review: Lesbian, Gay, Bisexual &
Legal Issues, 14, pp. 149–167.

U.S. Department of Health and Human Services, Administration for
Children and Families (2008). Evaluation of the life skills training program: Los Angeles County, Washington, D.C.

Wilbur, S. Ryan, C., Marksamer, J. (2006). CWLA best practices guidelines: Serving LGBT youth in out-of-home care. Child Welfare
League of America, Washington, DC.

Wolanin, T.R. (2005). Higher education opportunities for foster youth: A primer for policymakers. The Institute for Higher Education Policy, Washington, DC.

Yarbrough, Y. (2012). Information packet: LGBTQ youth permanency. National Center for Permanency and Family Connections. Silberman School of Social Work at Hunter College.

FOSTER FAMILY ACCEPTANCE

Understanding the Role of Foster Family Acceptance in the Lives of LGBTQ Foster Youth[1]

Adam McCormick, Kathryn Schmidt, and Samuel Terrazas

Family acceptance has been identified as one of the strongest predictors of the mental and behavioral health outcomes of LGBTQ youth. In fact, LGBTQ youth with accepting families are significantly less likely to attempt suicide and report experiencing depression. Additionally, LGBTQ youth who report high levels of family acceptance are much less likely to engage in risky behaviors such as unprotected sex and substance abuse. The current study was the first to look at the role that acceptance plays in the experiences of youth in foster care. Findings suggest that foster families who create accepting and affirming environments can have a profound impact on the experiences of LGBTQ youth in their care.

Foster care alumni (n = 26) were interviewed in this study in an attempt to compare the experiences of youth with accepting foster families to those who had rejecting experiences in foster care. Specific attention was given to their foster caretaker's willingness to acknowledge issues related to SOGIE, as well as their responses to experiences of mistreatment, bullying, or harassment. Findings suggest that LGBTQ youth with accepting foster parents were much more comfortable and safe in discussing intimate issues related to their sexuality and identity. In addition, youth in accepting families were much more likely to discuss other sensitive or intimate issues with their foster caretakers.

LGBTQ youth in care are much more likely to experience harassment and bullying from peers and adults. Findings from this study suggest that accepting foster caretakers were much more willing and equipped to address instances when LGBTQ youth are harassed or marginalized. Those LGBTQ youth in rejecting families were much more likely to remain silent about any experiences related to discrimination or bullying and much more likely to internalize those experiences.

The issue of double standards around dating, intimacy, and relationships has been documented in previous studies. Youth in this study with accepting families were much more likely to experience equity when it came to issues surrounding romantic relationships and extracurricular activities. In many cases, accepting families were much more likely to go out of their way to ensure that LGBTQ youth had access to friends and partners in the same ways that non-LGBTQ youth might. For LGBTQ youth in rejecting homes, many reported experiences of being discouraged or even prohibited from dating or attending events with other LGBTQ youth.

Foster families often experience minimal training that specifically addresses the need to create supporting and affirming environments for LGBTQ youth. Given the important role that family acceptance plays in the health and well-being of LGBTQ youth, it is critical that efforts to create a more inclusive and accepting system of care specifically address efforts to enhance foster family acceptance. Foster parents can play a critical role in helping to reinforce the idea that LGBTQ youth are deserving of a loving and affirming family.

Note

1 Reprinted with permission of Elsevier.

FOSTER FAMILY ACCEPTANCE

Understanding the Role of Foster Family Acceptance in the Lives of LGBTQ Youth

Adam McCormick, Kathryn Schmidt, and Samuel Terrazas

Children and Youth Services Review, 61 (2016) pp. 69–74

1. Introduction

LGBTQ youth in the child welfare system have historically received very little attention in the areas of practice, policy, and research. In fact, until recent years, little has been done to simply acknowledge the presence of LGBTQ youth in the child welfare system. While research addressing the experiences of LGBTQ youth in foster care has increased in recent years, these experiences suggest that the child welfare system is largely inadequate in fostering a culture of acceptance, safety, and affirmation (Mallon, 1998; Mallon, 1997; Woronoff & Estrada, 2006).

The limited research available on LGBTQ youth in care has been instrumental in highlighting many of the barriers that are often encountered in all aspects of the child welfare experience, from the point of contact all the way through to permanency. Although child welfare referrals may seem completely unrelated to a youth's sexual orientation or gender identity, referrals for LGBTQ youth often have much to do with both. Once they enter care, LGBTQ youth often experience harassment, incompetence, stigma, and rejection. These experiences largely contribute to placement instability, running away, social and emotional problems, and limited support networks. Little emphasis is placed on issues of permanency related services for LGBTQ youth, such as family reunification, adoption, and legal guardianship. Furthermore, child welfare professionals have largely relied upon more restrictive placements such as group homes and other congregate care settings when settling on placement options for LGBTQ youth (Mallon, 1998; Mallon, 1997; Woronoff & Estrada, 2006).

Despite all of the barriers and systemic flaws that LGBTQ youth often face in the child welfare system, Mallon, (1998), notes that this is a population that has much more resilience than risk. Furthermore, many professionals and stakeholders agree that efforts and initiatives aimed at creating more affirming policies and practices for LGBTQ youth in the child welfare system would significantly improve their lives and outcomes. An effort that has been strongly recommended in creating a more inclusive and affirming child welfare system for LGBTQ youth is the training and recruitment of foster families better equipped to meet the needs of LGBTQ youth (Wilber, Reyes, & Marksamer, 2006; Woronoff & Estrada, 2006

1.1. Review of the literature

1.1.1. ACKNOWLEDGMENT

One of the most significant challenges that has plagued the child welfare system is its inability to simply acknowledge the presence of LGBTQ youth. Many professionals and researchers credit this lack of visibility for largely contributing to many of the challenges that currently exist for LGBTQ youth in care (Mallon, 1998; Mallon, 1997; Woronoff & Estrada, 2006). Recent research suggesting that an openness and willingness to freely discuss issues related to sexual orientation and gender identity are both associated with positive outcomes for LGBTQ youth and young adults in their family systems makes this systemic lack of acknowledgment especially concerning (Ryan, Huebner, Diaz, & Sanches, 2009).

The child welfare system has been much more reluctant to foster awareness and dialogue around issues of sexual orientation and gender identity than many other youth serving systems. For instance, homeless, transitional, and runaway youth programs have historically had a much greater sense of comfort and willingness to acknowledge and address the presence and needs of LGBTQ youth and young adults who access their services.

1.1.2. PATHWAYS INTO CARE

The reasons that LGBTQ youth come into contact with the child welfare system are often very strongly related to issues pertaining to their sexual orientation or gender identity. Although these issues may not initially appear to have anything to do with a youth's sexual orientation or gender identity, after closer examination and exploration it is often the case that these issues influence a child's referral into the child welfare system. Many LGBTQ youth do, in fact, come into contact with the child welfare system for the same reasons as most straight youth (neglectful supervision, parental substance abuse, parental mental health, abuse, etc.). LGBTQ are, however, disproportionately overrepresented in cases of parental abandonment, runaways, truancy, and parental conflict (Mallon, 2011). Listening forums, interviews, and focus groups with LGBTQ teens and young adults suggest that many of these referrals stem from conflict pertaining to sexual orientation or gender identity. For instance, a parent who refuses to provide care to their child may be doing so because of conflict related to a family's refusal to accept the youth's sexual orientation or gender identity. Similarly, a child who is referred for reasons pertaining to truancy may be avoiding school for fears of being teased, bullied, rejected, or assaulted by peers. When asked, just under half of LGBTQ youth in care (44%) report that they were removed from their home for reasons that were somehow related to their sexual orientation or gender identity (Ryan & Diaz, 2009).

1.1.3. EXPERIENCES IN CARE

When LGBTQ youth enter the foster care system their experiences and living conditions do not always get better. In fact, previous research would suggest that in many cases they are entering a system that only seems to create more conflict, danger, rejection, and instability for LGBTQ youth Mallon, 1998; Mallon, 1997; Woronoff & Estrada, 2006).

Many LGBTQ youth in care report experiences of verbal and physical harassment, bullying, and isolation from peers. Furthermore, a strong theme that has emerged in previous research involves a dynamic in which LGBTQ youth are often blamed by caretakers and other child welfare professionals for the harassment and discrimination that they experience at the hands of their peers (Woronoff & Estrada, 2006). Caretakers often attribute the mistreatment experienced by LGBTQ youth to the fact that other youth are uncomfortable with or even offended by their sexual orientation or gender identify. Similarly, many caretakers will discourage LGBTQ youth from discussing their sexual orientation or romantic relationships with other youth which leads to social isolation and reinforces stigma.

Many LGBTQ youth in foster care view the streets as a less dangerous and hostile living situation than their current foster placements. Numerous research studies note the overrepresentation of LGBTQ youth in the homeless and runaway populations (Bailey, Camlin, & Ennett, 1998; Freeman & Hamilton, 2008; Gangamma, Slesnick, Toviessi, & Serovich, 2008). It is assumed that many of these homeless youth have at least some history of foster care placement during their childhood.

1.1.4. DOUBLE STANDARDS

Studies on the experiences of LGBTQ youth in the child welfare system have often referred to the double standards that exist between LGBTQ youth and straight youth (Woronoff & Estrada, 2006). In many cases, LGBTQ youth report that they are not provided with the same opportunities, privileges, and relationships that their straight counterparts are afforded. These double standards seem to be especially prevalent when it comes to friendships and romantic relationships. In some cases LGBTQ youth have reported being disciplined, even to the point of losing their placement, for engaging in age appropriate consensual same-sex relationships. Meanwhile, these same youth suggest that straight foster youth in their homes were allowed, in some cases even encouraged, to engage in romantic relationships with their opposite sex romantic partners. Similarly, many LGBTQ youth report being discouraged or prohibited from engaging in friendships with other LGBTQ youth and straight youth who affirm them.

1.1.5. PERMANENCY

The permanency process for many youth in foster care is challenging, however, there can be the potential for a number of additional challenges for LGBTQ youth in establishing permanency. Numerous studies suggest that there are a number of benefits that accompany an appropriate permanency outcome for youth in foster care (Fiermonte & Renne, 2002). Similarly, the inability to achieve permanency is often accompanied by social isolation and loneliness which often makes youth more vulnerable to discrimination, sexual abuse, and harassment (Jacobs & Freundlich, 2006). Such outcomes are especially troubling for many LGBTQ youth because their permanency options are often limited. Research suggests that LGBTQ youth are significantly less likely than their straight peers to achieve the most desired permanency outcomes of parental reunification and adoption (Mallon, 1997; Sullivan, 1994). In addition, LGBTQ youth are much less likely to have ties to their birth families and extended families (Mallon, 1997). Few services are available to LGBTQ youth and their families aimed at addressing any familial conflict that may be preventing family reunification. Similarly, little is done in terms of therapy and education to equip families to better identify the impact of both acceptance and rejection on their LGBTQ children. These services have a strong evidence base in other settings suggesting they help families to address and potentially change some of their perceptions, opinions, and beliefs related to their child's sexual orientation or gender identity (Ryan et al., 2009).

Placement in traditional foster care homes is typically the least restrictive option for youth when family reunification, kinship placements, or adoption are not possibilities. In many states, however, there is a critical shortage of foster families willing to provide an accepting and affirming environment for LGBTQ youth (Wilber et al., 2006). Similarly, many LGBTQ youth are reluctant to live in a family environment due in large part to their previous negative experiences with their own biological families. The lack of accepting foster families largely contributes to an overreliance on placing LGBTQ youth in group home and other congregate care settings primarily designated for youth with more severe behavioral and emotional needs (Woronoff & Estrada, 2006). Therefore, many LGBTQ youth are placed in settings that are much more restrictive than what is appropriate based upon their emotional and behavioral needs.

Many LGBTQ youth experience placement disruptions for behavioral reasons or relationship problems with peers and caretakers that stem from conflicts related to sexual orientation or gender identity (Mallon, 1997; Mallon, 1998; Woronoff & Estrada, 2006). Considering all of the factors and challenges associated with the placement and permanency of LGBTQ youth in foster care it is no surprise that they have a much higher rates of placement instability than straight youth. In fact, LGBTQ youth average 6.35 placements by the time that they achieve permanency, a rate that nearly doubles that of straight youth (Mallon, Aledort, & Ferrera, 2002).

2. Methods

A qualitative design was chosen for the current study in an attempt to both strengthen and further develop a theoretical understanding of family acceptance in the context of foster care. The current study project underwent a full review through the Institutional Review Board to ensure appropriate care of all subjects involved in study. While research with this population has largely focused on the experiences of LGBTQ youth in care (Mallon, 1998; Wilber et al., 2006; Woronoff & Estrada, 2006), no studies have specifically explored the role that foster family acceptance plays in the lives of youth as they navigate the child care system.

A comparative approach was utilized to compare the experiences of LGBTQ youth who identified accepting foster family experiences to those who identified rejecting foster family experiences. This comparative approach allowed the investigators to both further identify what acceptance and rejection look like within the foster care context, as well as to explore the benefits and consequences of each.

2.1. Procedures

The study sample was made up of alumni of the foster care system between the ages of 18–25. Participants (n = 26) completed 60–90 minute in-depth semi-structured qualitative interviews on their experiences with foster families while in care. Investigators used a structured interview guide that consisted of four main questions to serve as the scaffolding of the interview. The interview guide was developed in consultation with a group of researchers and practitioners from across the nation who were identified as having an expertise in working with LGBTQ youth in foster care. The group of experts used a combination of existing data and anecdotal professional experiences to identify a pool of potential questions and topics to explore with LGBTQ youth. From this pool of questions, the study's investigators chose four questions that they felt would be the best at allowing youth to discuss their experiences In addition, investigators used probing questions and follow-up questions in an attempt to further allow youth to provide depth, detail, thoughts and emotions to generate data that further explored their experiences. Interview questions addressed the following four areas:

1   Foster caretaker willingness and comfort in discussing and acknowledging issues related to sexual orientation.
2   Foster caretaker responses to mistreatment, harassment, and bullying of gay and lesbian youth.
3   Double standards that were experienced by gay and lesbian youth as compared to straight youth.
4   Youth descriptions of the ideal foster family for gay and lesbian youth in foster care.

Youth were also encouraged to discuss other relevant topics and experiences that pertained to the purpose and goals of the study.

2.2. Sample

The current study utilized a non-random availability sample of young adults with a history of foster care placement as children. Foster placement agencies, transitional youth programs, foster care alumni networks, and public child welfare agencies in Texas, Iowa, and Illinois were all used to recruit participants. The study announcement noted that any young adults (18–25) who identified as Lesbian, Gay, Bisexual, or Transgender with a history of public foster care placement during their childhood would be eligible to participate. A total of 26 participants were interviewed for the current study. No participants in the study identified as bisexual or transgender. The majority of participants (61%) identified as gay and male, while 39% identified as female and lesbian. The sample was largely made up of Caucasian participants (65%), with 24% identifying as African American and 11% as Latina/o. The mean age of participants in the study was 22.3. Participants were informed that interviews would likely be 60–90 min. No compensation was offered to subjects for participation in this study.

2.3. Data collection

The in-depth interviews were conducted by the lead author of this study. This individual has taught courses on qualitative research for a number of years and is well versed on topics such as data collection, building trust and rapport, interview administration, utilizing probing and follow-up questions to elicit in-depth and detailed responses, and debriefing.

Most of the interviews (23) were conducted in person. These interviews took place in private offices of child welfare agencies. The remaining interviews were conducted using the SKYPE telecommunications application software. To establish anonymity, participants were encouraged to only use their first name throughout the interview. All study participants completed a short debriefing process upon the completion of each interview and were provided an opportunity to ask the interviewer any questions that they might have. Similarly, participants were provided the opportunity to follow up on any comments that may have indicated emotional or psychological distress. None of the participants indicated that the interview caused them significant stress, although a few used the opportunity to reflect with the interviewer on difficult experiences from their foster care experience. Each interview was audio taped and transcribed by the authors of this study.

2.4. Data analysis

Thematic analysis of the data was conducted to identify relevant themes and patterns. This analysis also allowed for a more thorough interpretation of the data. An incident by incident coding technique was followed by a more extensive focused coding process to identify themes and patterns in the data.

The investigators performed a thorough review of all data to gain initial familiarity with the data set. When the initial review was complete and familiarity was established the investigators conducted a second review looking specifically at issues pertaining to foster family acceptance and participant experiences. Next, a preliminary thematic analysis was conducted to begin the process of identifying specific themes within the data. The final step included a more focused analysis of the themes initially identified to allow for the identification of larger themes and patterns.

3. Results

The following section presents a number of themes and patterns that emerged from the experiences of gay and lesbian foster care alumni as they pertain to foster family acceptance and rejection. While the qualitative methodology and small sample size in this study largely limit its generalizability, these findings do provide some insights into the role that foster family acceptance can play in the lives of gay and lesbian youth in foster care. Furthermore, these findings are the first to specifically compare the experiences of gay and lesbian youth with accepting foster family experiences to those who had rejecting experiences.

3.1. Acknowledgement

Participants identified a number of themes related to their foster caretakers' comfort and willingness to discuss and acknowledge issues pertaining to sexual orientation. Findings suggest that foster parents in accepting families exhibited a much greater sense of comfort in discussing issues related to sexual orientation. Similarly, participants with accepting foster family experiences expressed that accepting caretakers exhibited a heightened willingness to acknowledge the presence of LGBTQ youth in their care than those alumni in rejecting homes.

3.1.1. EMPOWERMENT

Participants often made reference to feelings and thoughts of empowerment and liberation when discussing a foster parent's willingness to acknowledge and discuss issues pertaining to sexual orientation, sexuality, gender expression and relationships. Several participants noted the sense of relief that they experienced when they no longer had to avoid conversations about these issues that were often uncomfortable or contentious. One participant noted this dynamic in the following quote, "They were the first people that actually sat down and talked to me about being gay. I was so surprised that I honestly didn't even know what to say. It was definitely a good thing for me at that time."

3.1.2. PATHWAY TO FURTHER DIALOGUE

A strong theme that emerged with participants who had foster parents willing to acknowledge and discuss issues pertaining to sexual orientation was that those experiences often opened the door to discuss issues related to sexual orientation and gender expression with other professionals. Many participants credited the open dialogue they had with their foster parents for their own willingness to initiate conversations with other professionals involved in their lives, including case workers, CASA workers, attorneys, and teachers. Similarly, many participants also cited their foster parents' willingness and ability to discuss issues pertaining to their sexual orientation as a catalyst for discussing other sensitive issues. One alumni shared the following statement when discussing the issue of acknowledgement, "I knew that if I could talk to them about stuff like my feelings and my boyfriend then there probably wasn't anything that I couldn't be open about." This theme was especially significant considering the many barriers and challenges to discussing sensitive and intimate topics that often exist for foster youth, regardless of their sexual orientation.

Participants in homes that they considered to be rejecting had significantly different experiences when it came to issues related to acknowledgment. While those in acknowledging homes cited dialogue as a catalyst for discussions on other sensitive or intimate topics, participants in homes where issues were not acknowledged often viewed this unwillingness to discuss issues as a barrier to discussing other intimate or sensitive topics. One youth stated, "The way she would avoid talking about made me shut down. How would I know that she wouldn't do the same thing when I tried to bring up other stuff."

Similarly, participants with caretakers who did not acknowledge or address issues related to sexual orientation also viewed this as a barrier to being open with other adults and professionals. This theme is present in the following statement, "I didn't want to say anything to my caseworker because I knew that they (foster parents) didn't like me talking about it. I didn't know if she would go back and tell them what I said."

3.1.3. SHAME AND INTERNALIZATION

Two alarming themes that emerged with participants in homes where issues were not acknowledged were shame and internalization of such attitudes. Many participants seemed to internalize the discomfort that their foster parents expressed. Subthemes that developed included a sense of loneliness due to the fact that they didn't have a healthy outlet and source of support, feelings of shame related to how they were perceived by their foster parents, and confusion related to how they felt as compared to how they were perceived and treated by foster parents.

One youth expanded on these feelings by stating, "The way they responded and avoided the issue made me feel like they were ashamed of me. When their family or friends would come over they come in my room and ask me if there were certain things that I planned on talking about."

Another participant stated, "At a time when I was feeling and thinking so much, there just wasn't anyone to talk to. I still really resent them for that."

3.2. Responses to mistreatment

One area in which participants with accepting experiences seemed to vary significantly from those who had rejecting experiences was in their foster parents' response to mistreatment, harassment, and bullying. A theme that emerged for alumni with accepting experiences was that their foster parents also served as advocates and activists when intervening on behalf of LGBTQ youth. Many participants discussed in great detail the efforts that their foster parents made to make sure that they were treated in the same ways as straight youth, whether in school or in the home. Furthermore, many of these participants shared what it meant to them that their caretakers were willing to stand up for them. When describing his former foster mother's response to a teacher who was not intervening when the youth was being bullied by peers, a participant shared the following, "She was irate. I was sitting outside the office and I could hear her yelling at him. It was nice to know that she felt that way. I think that it helped us to get along better."

Another participant stated, "We would joke that she was going to get a bumper sticker on her car that said her child had perfect attendance at the high school gay-straight alliance."

Participants in rejecting families had much different experiences with their foster parents when they approached them about mistreatment they were experiencing. A very strong and consistent theme that emerged with this group was blame and responsibility for any mistreatment, bullying, and/or harassment that they experienced. Many participants noted that when their foster parents were made aware of mistreatment they often attributed it to issues related to the youth's sexual orientation. This theme is evidenced in the following statement by a young man explaining an incident in which his group of friends were beginning to withdraw from him, "She asked me if I thought that they might be on to something and maybe they were just trying to help me to know that they didn't want to have anything to do with me if I was that way." Others described a dynamic in which foster parents were indifferent to the ways that they might have been mistreated by peers or teachers. One participant noted,

It was like she didn't even care that my life was a living hell when I was at school. I remember being in tears one morning trying to convince her to not make me go back or to do something about it. She never did.

3.3. Double standards

Findings suggest that youth in rejecting families were much more likely to encounter double standards when it came to friendships, romantic relationships, and extracurricular interests.

3.3.1. EFFORTS TO CONNECT YOUTH WITH AFFIRMING PEERS

Many participants in accepting families mentioned the lengths that their foster parents went to in attempts to help facilitate and maintain friendships with affirming peers and other LGBTQ youth. Many of these foster parents made efforts to connect youth with programs or groups such as gay-straight alliances or drop in centers. Additionally, a strong theme that emerged was that participants felt that they experienced no difference than straight youth when it came to things like going to a friend's house, curfews, and having friends over. When discussing his foster father's approach to having friends over one participant stated, "He made it clear right away that my friends were just as welcome as anyone else's."

In addition, youth in accepting homes had much more freedom and independence to socialize with friends outside of the home. This theme is emphasized in the following statement, "I think she was so happy that I was making friends that she would do anything to help support it, even if it meant driving across town to take me places."

Findings suggest that youth with rejecting experiences had vastly different experiences when it came to how their foster parents dealt with their peer relationships. Many were discouraged from engaging in friendships with peers who their foster parents deemed to be supportive of their sexual orientation. Another theme that emerged was that many participants felt that their foster parents largely monitored who they were spending time with as noted in the following comment, "They were always looking into who I was hanging out with and they would even ask the other kids in the house if my friends were gay."

3.3.2. APPROACHES TO ROMANTIC RELATIONSHIPS

A number of themes emerged when comparing the approaches to romantic relationships that participants experienced. A consistent theme for those with accepting experiences was that their foster parents had the same standards about things like dating, physical affection, and having romantic partners for LGBTQ youth as they did for straight youth. When explaining the intake meeting that he had when he was first placed in his foster home, one participant shared the following encounter,

My caseworker mentioned to them (foster parents) that I had a boyfriend back home that I would really like to visit sometime. I didn't expect them to be okay with that and my caseworker even told me on the drive over that it was unlikely. But, they were totally cool with it and they actually followed through several times and we would meet his parents halfway.

In contrast, romantic relationships were largely discouraged and in many cases even forbidden for many participants who had rejecting experiences. Participants often mentioned that they did not have the same rights and privileges as straight youth when it come to things like dating and physical affection. This theme is underscored in the following participant comment,

The other kids could practically get to second base with their boyfriends on the living room couch when we would have movie night, but I couldn't even think about having a girl over. Unless, of course, she was coming over as a friend. So, I would say she was just a friend.

3.4. The ideal foster family

When asked to describe the ideal foster family for a gay or lesbian teen the characterizations and explanations were very similar for both the participants who had accepting experiences and those who had rejecting experiences. The most prevalent and consistent theme that emerged from this question was that ideal foster families need to be accepting and affirming. Participants were able to both articulate and explain the reasons why acceptance is of such importance, as well as to illustrate its positive impact. When probed about what acceptance would ideally look like, participants often cited things like being non-judgmental, having an openness to new things and ideas, and valuing a youth's differences.

One theme that arose in many interviews was that many LGBTQ participants are willing to overlook the shortcomings of foster families if they are simply willing to accept their sexual orientation. This theme was emphasized in the following statement, "I didn't care if they were too strict or that they did other things that drove me crazy. They accepted that I was gay and I knew that I wasn't going to do anything to mess this placement up."

In addition to acceptance, participants also mentioned communication as being one of the most important characteristics when describing the ideal foster family. Participants stressed the importance of having an open and honest dialogue about issues, as well as the potential positive impact that this communication can have on youth. When probed about what she would tell a prospective foster parent about how to approach LGBTQ youth, one participant stated, "Just talk to them about stuff. Don't just think that they can assume things about you and how you feel because a lot of us assume the worst."

3.5. Implications for practice, research and policy

The current study provides some important new insights into the significance of family acceptance, as well as the profound impact that it can have on the well-being and stability of LGBTQ youth in care. Findings from this study have a number of practical implications for policymakers, child welfare professionals, and caretakers.

Education and training on the role that family acceptance has on LGBTQ youth in foster care can likely play a significant role in improving foster parent approaches to youth. Research with LGBTQ young adults in the general population suggests that parents and caretakers who are aware of the consequences that rejection can have on their loved ones are much likely to change any behaviors or parenting approaches that resemble rejection (Ryan et al., 2009). Although the relationship dynamics often differ significantly in a foster family setting more traditional families, there is reason to believe that many foster parents would be less inclined to exhibit rejecting behaviors if they are aware of the negative ways in which they can impact vulnerable youth. As public and private child welfare agencies begin to acknowledge the presence of LGBTQ youth, training underscoring the importance of acceptance would likely go a long way in increasing the amount of awareness and acknowledgement of these populations. Similarly, education on the specific behaviors and activities associated with acceptance would likely be an empowering and informing resource for existing and potential foster parents and child welfare professionals.

In addition to increased training on the importance of foster family acceptance for foster caretakers and child welfare professionals, the current study provides further evidence of the need for more affirming and accepting foster parents for LGBT youth. The limited research related to permanency issues for LGBTQ youth emphasizes the many challenges that exist in finding placements that are affirming, accepting, and inclusive. More simply put, in many parts of the nation it is much more difficult to find a foster placement in which caretakers are accepting of LGBTQ youth than to find one that is not. Efforts to recruit families who embody the characteristics and qualities conveyed by young adults in this study such as acceptance, open mindedness, and the ability to openly communicate about sensitive issues related to sexuality, sexual orientation, and gender expression would certainly have a profound impact on the experiences of LGBTQ youth. The current climate throughout society appears to suggest that people are more open and accepting of LGBTQ youth than we were at any other time. Legal marriage and growing acceptance for gay and lesbian adults also reduces barriers to their recruitment as foster parents. Child welfare professionals would likely benefit from this shift in attitudes, perceptions, and beliefs about LGBTQ youth.

The current study has a number of implications for future research and policy. The findings suggest that foster family acceptance has the potential to play a pivotal role in the experiences of LGBTQ youth. There is currently no research available exploring the experience and readiness of foster caregivers to provide affirming and accepting care. Future research aimed at assessing the challenges and barriers that foster families exhibit would likely help to aid training, recruitment, and education efforts. Furthermore, research exploring families who have been effective in creating safe, inclusive, and accepting homes for LGBTQ youth would likely help practitioners and policy makers have a more accurate and extensive understanding of what accepting care should look like.

California was the first state to adopt a statewide antidiscrimination policy aimed at improving the experiences of LGBTQ youth. To date, there are no federal efforts specifically addressing discrimination of LGBTQ youth. The current study provides further evidence of the need for policy initiatives that mandate states to protect LGBTQ youth in care through the training and recruitment of sensitive and affirming caregivers. Furthermore, LGBTQ youth in care would likely benefit significantly from policy efforts that enhance the recruitment and screening process for foster families by assessing a caretaker's level of readiness and competence to work with LGBTQ youth.

4. Conclusion

The challenges and obstacles that many LGBTQ youth face as they navigate the child welfare system are robust and can be devastating at times. This is clearly evident in the limited research available noting that the experiences of LGBTQ youth often worsen after they enter the child welfare system. Furthermore, LGBTQ youth experience placement disruption at alarming rates and their permanency options have historically been limited to long term care in congregate care settings until they age out of foster care. Despite all of these challenges, LGBTQ youth in foster care continue to be a population with far more resilience and resourcefulness than risk. The current study sheds some light on the role that foster family acceptance can have in helping to foster that sense of resilience to improve the experiences and opportunities for LGBTQ youth.

The child welfare system is slowly becoming more responsive to the needs of LGBTQ youth. Understanding the role that foster acceptance plays in meeting those needs and better operationalizing what acceptance looks like in the context of foster care can play a pivotal role in this response. The current study conveys the experiences of foster care alumni who clearly have meaningful and thoughtful insights into the vital role that foster family acceptance can play in the lives of LGBTQ youth as they navigate the foster care experience.

References

Bailey, S. L., Camlin, C. S., & Ennett, S. T. (1998). Substance use and risky sexual behavior among homeless and runaway youth. Journal of Adolescent Health, 23, 378–388.

Fiermonte C., & Renne, J. L. (2002). Making it permanent: Reasonable efforts to finalize permanency plans for foster children. Retrieved from https://www.americanbar.org/groups/child_law/publications.html

Freeman, L., & Hamilton, D. (2008). A count of homeless youth in New York City. New York: Empire State Coalition of Youth and Family Services. Available at: http://www.citylimits.org/images_pdfs/pdfs/HomelessYouth.pdf

Gangamma, R., Slesnick, N., Toviessi, P., & Serovich, J. (2008). Comparison of HIV risks among gay, lesbian, bisexual, and heterosexual homeless youth. Journal of Youth and Adolescence, 37, 456–464.

Jacobs, J., & Freundlich, M. (2006). Achieving permanency for LGBTQ youth. Child Welfare, 85(2), 299–316.

Mallon, G. P. (1997). Toward a competent child welfare service delivery system for gay and lesbian adolescents and their Families. Journal of Multicultural Social Work, 5(3/4), 177–194.

Mallon, G. P. (1998). We don't exactly get the Welcome Wagon: The experiences of gay and lesbian adolescents in child welfare systems. New York: Columbia University Press.

Mallon, G. P. (2011). The home study assessment process for gay, lesbian, bisexual, and transgender prospective foster and adoptive families. Journal of GLBT Family Studies, 7(1/2), 9–29.

Mallon, G. P., Aledort, N., & Ferrera, M. (2002). There's no place like home: Achieving safety, permanency, and well-being for lesbian and gay adolescents in out-of home care settings. Child Welfare, 81(2), 407–439.

Ryan, C., & Diaz, R. (2009). *FAP Risk Assessment Tool*. San Francisco: Family Acceptance Project, San Francisco State University.

Ryan, C., Huebner, D., Diaz, R. M., & Sanches, J. (2009). Family Rejection as a predictor of negative health outcomes in white and Latino lesbian, gay, and bisexual young adults. Pediatrics, 123(1), 346–352.

Sullivan, T. (1994). Obstacles to effective child welfare service with gay and lesbian youth. Child Welfare, 73(4), 291–304.

Wilber, S., Reyes, C., & Marksamer, J. (2006). The Model Standards Project: Creating inclusive systems for LGBT youth in out-of-home care. Child Welfare, 85(2), 133–149.

Woronoff, R., & Estrada, R. (2006). Regional listening forums: An examination of the methodologies used by the Child Welfare League of America and Lambda Legal to highlight the experiences of LGBTQ youth in care. Child Welfare, 85(2), 341–360.

REFERENCES

Association for Children and Families. (2015). *A national look at congregate care in child welfare*. Retrieved from: www.acf.hhs.gov/sites/default/files/cb/cbcongregatecare_brief.pdf

Brown, B. (2006). Shame resilience theory: A grounded theory study on women and shame. *Families in Society, 87*(1), 43–52.

California Welfare and Institutions Code section 458. (2004). California Legislative Council. Retrieved from: http://leginfo.legislature.ca.gov/faces/billNavClient.xhtml?bill_id=200320040AB458

Centers for Disease Control and Prevention. (2011). Sexual identity, sex of sexual contacts, and health-risk behaviors among students in grades 9–12—Youth Risk Behavior Surveillance, selected sites, United States, 2001–2009. *MMWR, 60*(7), 1–133.

Dank, M., Lachman, P., Yahner, J., & Zweig, J. (2014). Dating violence of lesbian, gay, bisexual, and transgender youth. *Journal of Youth Adolescence, 43,* 846–853.

Dank, M., Yahner, J., Madden, K., Banuelos, I., Yu, L., Ritchie, A., Mora, M., & Conner, B. (2015). *Surviving the streets of New York: Experiences of LGBTQ youth, YMSM, and YWSW engaged in survival sex*. Washington, D.C.: Urban Institute Research Report.

Durso, L.E., & Gates, G.J. (2012). *Serving our youth: Findings from a national survey of service providers working with lesbian, gay, bisexual, and transgender youth who are homeless or at risk of becoming homeless*. Los Angeles: The Williams Institute with True Colors Fund and The Palette Fund.

Estrada, R., & Marksamer, J. (2006). The legal rights of LGBT youth in state custody: What child welfare and juvenile justice professionals need to know. *Child Welfare, 85*(2), 171–194.

Friedman, M.S., Marshal, M.P., Guadamuz, T.E., Wei, C., Wong, C., Saewyc, E., & Stall, R. (2011). A meta-analysis to examine disparities in childhood physical and sexual abuse among sexual and non-sexual minorities. *American Journal of Public Health,* *101*(8), 1481–1494.

Garofalo, R., Deleon, J., Osmer, E., Doll, M., & Harper, G. (2006). Overlooked, misunderstood and at-risk: Exploring the lives of HIV risk ethnic minority male-to-female transgender youth. *Journal of Adolescent Health, 38*(3), 230–236.

Grossman, A.H., & D'Augeli, A.R. (2007). Transgender youth and life threatening behaviors. *Suicide and Life Threatening Behavior, 37*(5), 527–537.

Haas, A.P., Rodgers, P.L., Herman, J.L. (2014). *Suicide attempts among transgender and gender non-conforming adults: Findings of the national transgender discrimination survey.* New York, NY and Los Angeles, CA: American Foundation for Suicide Prevention and Williams Institute, UCLA School of Law.

H.R. 4980. (2014). Preventing Sex Trafficking and Strengthening Families Act. 113th United States Congress 113–183.

Kosciw, J.G., Greytak, E.A., Palmer, N.A., & Boesen, M.J. (2013). *The 2013 National School Climate Survey: The experiences of lesbian, gay, bisexual and transgender youth in our nation's schools.* New York: GLSEN.

Liu, R., & Mustanski, B. (2012). Suicidal ideation and self-harm in lesbian, gay, bisexual, and transgender youth. *American Journal of Preventive Medicine, 42*(3), 221–228.

Lutnick, A. (2016). *Domestic minor sex trafficking: Beyond victims and villains.* New York, NY: Columbia University Press.

Mallon, G.P. (1998). *We don't exactly get the Welcome Wagon: The experiences of gay and lesbian adolescents in child welfare systems.* New York: Columbia University Press.

Mallon, G.P. (2011). The home study assessment process for gay, lesbian, bisexual, and transgender prospective foster and adoptive families. *Journal of GLBT Family Studies, 7*(1/2), 9–29.

Mallon, G.P., Aledort, N., & Ferrera, M. (2002). There's no place like home: Achieving safety, permanency, and well-being for lesbian and gay adolescents in out-of home care settings. *Child Welfare, 81*(2), 407–443.

Mallon, G.P., & Woronoff, R. (2006). Busting out of the child welfare closet: Lesbian, gay, bisexual, and transgender-affirming approaches to child welfare. *Child Welfare 85*(2), 115–122.

Marshal, M.P., Friedman, M.S., Stall, R., King, K.M., Miles, J., Gold, M.A., et al. (2008). Sexual orientation and adolescent substance use: A meta-analysis and methodological review. *Addiction, 103*(4), 546–556.

McCormick, A., Schmidt, K., & Clifton, E. (2015). Gay straight alliances: Understanding their role and impact on the academic experiences of LGBT students. *Children in Schools, 37*(2), 65–128.

McCormick, A., Schmidt, K., & Terrazas, S. (2016). Foster family acceptance: Understanding the role of foster family acceptance for LGBTQ youth in care. *Children and Youth Services Review, 61,* 69–74.

Mitchum, P., & Moodie Mills, A. (2014). *Beyond bullying: How hostile school climates perpetuate the school to prison pipeline for LGBTQ youth.* Washington, DC: The Center for American Progress.

NCTSN Core Curriculum on Childhood Trauma Task Force. (2012). *The 12 core concepts: Concepts for understanding traumatic stress responses in children and families. Core Curriculum on Childhood Trauma.* Los Angeles, CA and Durham, NC: UCLA-Duke University National Center for Child Traumatic Stress.

Roberts, A., Rosario, M., Corliss, H.L., Koenen, K.C., & Austin, S.B. (2012a). Elevated risk of post traumatic stress in sexual minority youths: Mediation by childhood abuse and gender nonconformity. *American Journal of Public Health, 102*(8), 1587–1593.

Roberts, A., Rosario, M., Corliss, H.L., Koenen, K.C., & Austin, S.B. (2012b). Childhood gender nonconformity: A risk indicator for childhood abuse and posttraumatic stress in youth. *Pediatrics, 129*(3), 410–417.

Russell, S.T., Toomey, R.B., Ryan, C., & Diaz, R.M. (2014). Being out at school: The implications for school victimization and young adult adjustment. *American Journal of Orthopsychiatry, 84*(6), 635–643. doi: 10.1037/ort0000037

Ryan, C., & Diaz, R. (2005). *FAP risk assessment tool.* San Francisco: Family Acceptance Project, San Francisco State University.

Ryan, C., Huebner, D., Diaz, R.M., & Sanches, J. (2009). Family rejection as a predictor of negative health outcomes in white and Latino lesbian, gay, and bisexual young adults. *Pediatrics, 123*(1), 346–352.

Shilo, G., & Savaya, R. (2011). Effects of family and friend support on LGB youth mental health and sexual orientation milestones. *Family Relations, 60*(3), 318–330.

Substance Abuse and Mental Health Services Administration. (2015). *Ending conversion therapy: Supporting and affirming LGBTQ youth.* HHS Publication No. (SMA) 15–4928. Rockville, MD: Substance Abuse and Mental Health Services Administration.

Wilson, B., Cooper, K., Kastanis, A., & Nezhad, S. (2014). Sexual and gender minority youth in foster care: Addressing disproportionality and disparities in Los Angeles. Retrieved from: http://william-sinstitute.law.ucla.edu/wp-content/uploads/LAFYS_report_final-aug-2014.pdf

Wilson, H., & Widom, C.S. (2010). Does physical abuse, sexual abuse, or neglect in childhood increase the likelihood of same-sex sexual relations and cohabitation. *Archives of Sexual Behavior, 39*(1), 63–74.

Woronoff, R., & Estrada, R. (2006). Regional listening forums: An examination of the methodologies used by the Child Welfare league of America and Lambda Legal to highlight the experiences of LGBTQ Youth in Care. *Child Welfare, 85*(2), 341–360.

INDEX